SETTING
THE CAPTIVES
FREE!

SETTING
THE
CAPTIVES
FREE!

Relevant Ideas in
Criminal Justice
& Prison Ministry

Don Smarto, Editor

BAKER BOOK HOUSE
Grand Rapids, Michigan 49516

Published by Baker Book House Company
P.O. Box 6287, Grand Rapids, Michigan 49516-6287

Printed in the United States of America

Library of Congress Cataloging-in-Publication Data

Smarto, Donald
    Setting the captives free! : relevant ideas in criminal justice and prison ministry / Donald Smarto, editor.
       p. cm.
    Papers from the National Prison Ministry Conference held June 1991 at Wheaton College, Wheaton, Ill.
    ISBN 0-8010-8337-0
    1. Church work with prisoners. 2. Church work with criminals. I. Smarto, Donald. II. National Prison Ministry Conference (1991 : Wheaton College)
BV4340.S475 1993
259′.5—dc20   92-42047

To Gloria and Bill Beyers
my mother- and father-in-law
who have consistently encouraged me
to serve Christ and his kingdom, first.

Contents

Part Four
Seeking Justice

Part Five
The Future of Prison Ministry

Acknowledgments

I want to thank the national leaders and speakers of the 1991 National Prison Ministry Conference at Wheaton College for making this work possible.

My appreciation to Lorraine Thompson, who spent hours transcribing audio tapes and typing these messages.

Introduction

This book features the collected wisdom of the key leaders in America's prison ministry today. Its list of contributors reads as a "who's who" in the most vigorous and dynamic effort to bring Christ's message to prisoners that our country has ever witnessed.

The articles were edited from speeches delivered at the National Prison Ministry Conference held June 1991 at Wheaton College, Wheaton, Illinois. This was a momentous event, only the second time in history that the many different prison ministry groups had gathered for a national conference. The first such conference had been held only five years earlier, in June of 1986.

Hosting both conferences was the Institute for Prison Ministries, begun in 1984 as a program of the Billy Graham Center. Since its inception, this organization has served as a catalyst to network the nearly five hundred jail and prison ministries across the country. It also provides training courses and research to help raise the level of professionalism among those who work in these ministries.

Prior to the formation of the Institute, the many diverse groups who minister to prisoners had little opportunity to share concerns and strategies. Roman Catholic, mainline Protestant, charismatic, and nondenominational groups were involved in a variety of efforts, from frontline evangelism to discipling and aftercare, but each group tended to keep to itself. Charismatic groups gathered together every year. The Salvation Army held annual correctional services meetings. Prison Fellowship, the largest prison ministry movement in the world, pulled its staff together periodically for retreats and training. But not until the forming of the Institute for Prison Ministries and the convening of the 1986 national conference did the movement toward greater unity begin.

All Christian ministries, of course, have a biblical basis for coming together under the lordship and authority of Christ, and it should be natural for ministries with similar goals to work together. Unfortunately, this has not always been the case. In prison ministries, as in other ministries, territorialism, competition, and an accentuation of differences have kept people apart and hindered the Lord's work.

But change is in the air! In the past decade, those who minister in different organizations and address different areas of concern have felt a deep need to work together, to help each other, and learn from each other. This is what made the June 1991 conference especially significant in a historical sense. I am grateful to Baker Book House for giving those who were unable to attend this important event—both those in prison ministries and the church at large—the opportunity to benefit from this growing spirit of cooperation.

In this book, then, you will share in the combined efforts of men and women who are dedicated to bringing the gospel of Jesus Christ to prisons; men and women of great vision and courage, many of whom I would call modern-day prophets. Men and women from ministries representing more than sixty thousand volunteers who share the gospel with prisoners on a regular basis.

Why is the message of this book important? First, because problems of crime and corrections are reaching crisis proportions in our nation. In the past decade we have become the most violent society in the world, and the incarceration rate has skyrocketed.

At the time of the 1986 conference, for example, California reported more than 55,000 inmates. By the time of the 1991 conference, that number had climbed to 100,000. In 1986, the United States had the third highest per capita rate of incarceration in the world. By 1991, we had moved ahead of the Soviet Union and South Africa to number-one spot! In 1986, 584,000 inmates crowded American prisons. Today we have more than a million—a 200 percent increase in less than ten years.

The average new prison costs approximately sixty million dollars, and we are spending four times as much on new prison construction as we are spending on education. In some states it costs twenty-five thousand dollars a year to house an inmate. The burden on the taxpayer will be devastating if these numbers continue to climb.

In spite of this proliferation of prisons, however, crime is on the increase. Drugs menace our society, particularly our youth. Gang violence is on the increase in the suburbs as well as the cities. Without a doubt, everything that government has tried to do in corrections has been like a Band-Aid on a ruptured artery. Although many fine administrators in corrections facilities are doing their best, clearly their best is not good enough.

That is one reason this book is important—because the issue of crime and corrections is one that we must face as a nation. Those of us in the body of Christ, however, have another reason for focusing our attention on prison ministries. We as Christians have a specific biblical mandate to reach out to prisoners. Evangelism is not an elective for us—and it cannot be selective. We are to have a burden for the lost, which includes the lepers of our society, the criminals.

The messages of this book are riveting and straightforward. They come from men and women who have reflected on the Scriptures, who have frontline experiences in America's jails and prisons, and who have led a virtual army of volunteers to minister to men and women behind bars. I hope that their voices in this book will encourage and challenge you.

Don Smarto

Part 1

Crimes and
Victims of Crimes

Introduction

In the 7 October 1991 issue of *U.S. News and World Report,* editor David Gergen noted that 500 people had died that year in the civil strife in Yugoslavia. During the same period, he pointed out, violence in the county of Los Angeles had resulted in nearly 1,500 deaths.

I come from a Sicilian family who knew Al Capone, socialized with his notorious bodyguards Alberto Anselmi and John Scalise, and entertained Capone's rivals, the five brutal Genna brothers. These Prohibition-era gangsters have come to epitomize ruthless violence to many people. And yet Chicago, the city Al Capone made famous for gangland slayings, sees more violence today than at the height of the Mafia wars. In the ten years between 1924 and 1934, the gangland wars between Capone, "Bugs" Moran, the Genna brothers, and Dion O'Bannion resulted in 500 deaths. Yet the single year 1991 saw more than 845 murders in Chicago—most the result of gang activity and illegal drug deals.

During the Persian Gulf War, 376 Americans died. During the same period, nearly 1,600 people were killed on the streets of New York City.

A Week in Our Cities

What do these numbers tell us? Our cities are riddled with crime, and the ranks of crime victims are swelling. As President Bush pointed out in his 28 January 1992 State of the Union address, "Victims of crime need our attention. When the average citizen is afraid to walk in a park his taxes paid for, then his civil rights are being violated."

To demonstrate the magnitude of the problem, let me describe a single week in our country's crime history from a personal perspective. Between 12 and 18 October 1991, I traveled to three American cities and witnessed the dramatic impact of crime on the everyday life of their citizens.

On Saturday, 12 October, I arrived in New York City, where I would speak in three churches the following day. After landing at LaGuardia Airport and checking into my hotel, I took a subway ride from Queens to Manhattan at eleven in the morning. During the twenty-minute ride, I observed the other riders in my subway car. It was daylight, yet everyone looked fearful and insecure. No one smiled. No one made eye contact with anyone else. The three women riders clutched their purses tightly against them. With every stop and the entrance of a new rider, most passengers glanced up fearfully toward the stranger. The ride, however, was without incident.

I got off the subway at Grand Central Station. Before noon, I entered a restroom at the station. I had been in the restroom for only three to five seconds when I saw a drug exchange in open view. Next a man exposed himself and made a crude sexual remark to me. A heated verbal exchange led to a man physically attacking another man. I did not stay in the restroom more than three minutes and yet during that time I observed at least three crimes: (1) possession of illegal drugs, (2) assault and battery, and (3) a sexual offense.

After two hours in downtown Manhattan, I decided to take a bus back to my hotel. On the bus driver's radio I heard this newscast: "In Brooklyn today, an armed man forced his way into a children's birthday party and attempted to steal wallets, jewelry, and valuables. The would-be robber was shot with his own gun by an adult at the party." With that final announcement, a cheer went up from many of the people riding the bus. One woman sitting next to me said, "It's about time we win one!" The elation of my fellow passengers made me realize that they considered any form of justice a rarity.

The next day, Sunday, I was scheduled to speak in three churches, beginning with the Manhattan Grace Tabernacle Church in Harlem. At six-thirty that morning, on a subway platform not far from the church, a fifty-nine-year-old man named

Leandro Rosebro was waiting for the train. Another man attempted to rob him. When Leandro resisted, the mugger threw him off the subway platform. Leandro was crushed under the wheels of an oncoming train. The mugger escaped without capture.

I arrived at Manhattan Grace Tabernacle Church to the sounds of auto alarms going off in the distance. The sidewalk was littered with safety glass. I watched my driver put a large metal locking device on his steering column—although it was only ten in the morning on a busy public street—then activate his own auto alarm.

The church, which was meeting on the second floor of an old warehouse building, bristled with protective devices—TV cameras, bars on windows, and electronic alarms. The main door to the sanctuary, which had probably been used for storage at one time, was made of thick metal with a large fortress-type bolt.

As we drove to the second church, Christ Tabernacle Church in Brooklyn, I heard on the car radio that a forty-seven-year-old New Yorker, Albert Brooks, had opened fire in a house. He had killed his father and three other people and critically wounded two neighbors, then taken hostages in the house he entered in Great Neck, Long Island. A neighbor was interviewed: "They were all his friends. This is a quiet neighborhood. It is not like there are problems around here." He had no record of prior arrest or any history of mental problems.

The police and Brooks were at a stalemate as the service began at Christ Tabernacle. By six in the evening, when the service concluded, I heard that Albert Brooks had shot himself in the head with a sawed-off rifle rather than surrender to police.

My third church was the Brooklyn Tabernacle on Flatbush Avenue in Brooklyn. The pastor, Jim Cymbala, began the seven-thirty service with an announcement about a sixteen-year-old who had accepted the Lord only five days before. He announced to the congregation that the youth had been stabbed twenty-two times at a subway station not far from the church. He had survived, but his condition was critical.

The next day, Monday, 14 October, I left New York and arrived in Washington, D.C. for a series of meetings. That morning I heard a radio news report that a gun had been fired in the halls of Calvin Senior High School—the fifth report of gunfire in a

Washington, D.C. high school in one month. Inspector Melvin Clark of the Fourth Police District stated that two groups of students had argued over a girl. The next day, Tuesday, 15 October, I read in the *Washington Post* that the Washington, D.C. school board urged putting metal detectors in all the high schools and junior highs in Washington, D.C.

According to the Children's Defense Fund reporting in *USA Today* in 1990, 135,000 children bring a gun to school each day. On any given day, 1,629 children are in adult jails.

I visit Washington, D.C. frequently. I have seen the covered bodies of shoot-out victims on sidewalks and in cars. It is a sobering sight.

The newspaper also featured an interview with YMCA worker Raymond Epps explaining how the children of Washington, D.C. "grow up too fast." He said, "they know too much. You've got to expose these kids to a lot of positive things. If you don't, they will just pick up off the streets." He told of one particular child, ten-year-old Devina Harper, who was robbed of her lunch money in the first week at school and subsequently chased by a youth with a gun. On a recent Saturday morning, while watching cartoons on her TV, Devina looked out her bedroom window to see a man walking down the street with blood covering his face as a result of a bad drug deal. Devina said her favorite TV shows are *Cops* and *America's Most Wanted* because "I like to hear about the fugitives. . . . They look so familiar."

Janice Williams, executive director of the Washington YMCA added, "The thing that amazes me is that they get over it so fast." She said children talk with nonchalance about street crimes as if they were talking about the *Cosby Show* or *The Simpsons*. Almost daily, these kids watch drug deals, see people getting shot, or experience robberies. They are victims of crime both directly and indirectly. They become desensitized to violence and murder. They also experience abuse, both physical and sexual at an alarming rate in urban ghettos.

On the ten o'clock news, I watched a report on the continuation of a wave of armed robberies in Washington, D.C. stores. Early that evening, twenty-five customers were ordered to lie on the floor on the four-hundred block of Fourteenth Street, near Capitol Hill. The TV report went on to say that in the first nine months of 1991 there had been thirty-five armed robberies in close proximity to Constitution Avenue and Independence Avenue—the neighborhood of the U.S. Supreme Court building, the Capitol building, the National Archives, the historical monuments, and the White House. In the city as a whole, during the first six months of 1991, there had been 3,646 armed robberies—most of them in grocery stores. I have seen stores in D.C. with armed police stationed inside.

I returned to Chicago on Wednesday, 16 October. As I walked through the air terminal of O'Hare Airport, newsstand headlines reported that twelve youths had been injured in a spray of gang-related gunfire. In the five days I had been gone, six young people had died in Chicago due to crime activity.

I have met with Chicago gang members who have lost dozens of fellow gang members through senseless violence. Gordon McLean, a Christian who works with gangs, told me, "I attend far more funerals than weddings."

I made my way home, unpacked, and tried to relax in front of the television—only to be bombarded with reports of more violence. A man had crashed his truck into a cafeteria in the small town of Killeen, Texas and then shot twenty-two people to death. It was, the reporter noted, the worst mass attack shooting in U.S. history.

The week ended Friday, 18 October, with a feature newspaper story in the *Chicago Tribune* about Jeffrey Dahmer, the Milwaukee man who had confessed to killing seventeen boys and men between 1978 and 1991. As trial preparation continued, it was disclosed that Dahmer had dismembered his victims and even eaten parts of them. And twelve of these murders had occurred shortly after Dahmer's release from prison. He had been convicted of molesting a thirteen-year-old boy. He had served only ten months. At the time of his sentencing, Circuit Court Judge William D. Gardner had predicted, with chilling accuracy, that Dahmer would come out "worse than you are right now."

An Epidemic of Fear

What did I learn from observing the week of crime in America? First, I realized with fresh intensity the anger and fear that stalks

American streets. Being a suburbanite, I sometimes fail to grasp the daily tension that urban dwellers—especially the poor—experience at almost every turn.

Many of our American cities are truly as dangerous and as fear-ridden as any war zone in the world. And although many of those killed or injured by urban violence are "druggies" and gang members, many more are innocent victims such as the young deaf girl in the summer of 1991 who was signing goodbye to her boyfriend. She signed "I love you." Gang members in a passing car, mistaking her gesture for the hand signal of a rival gang, shot and killed her.

Cities seem to be primary incubation centers for violence these days. And yet even our suburbs and small towns are not immune to this contagion of fear—as the Killeen, Texas, killings indicate. In a sense, the stress of living under such conditions makes victims of us all.

In October 1991, a graduate student from China who was studying at the University of Iowa killed two professors, two administrators, a fellow student, and himself. A fellow Chinese student observed in *USA Today* that such an incident "is not in the Chinese tradition: a sense of collective responsibility." The student said, "My first response was, 'He's very American now.'"

What did that student mean? Is that the way people who are jealous, depressed, or distraught resolve their difficulties in our country—by killing innocent people? A look at our recent history suggests disturbing answers.

In 1983, thirteen people die in a robbery in Seattle's Chinatown.

In 1984, a gunman opens fire in a McDonald's restaurant in San Ysidro, California. A significant number of the twenty-one people killed were children.

In 1986, a disgruntled postal worker opens fire in a post office in Edmund, Oklahoma, killing fourteen people.

In 1987, Gene Simmons shoots sixteen people, including fourteen members of one family, in rural Arkansas.

In 1988, a woman opens fire on a schoolyard in northern Illinois, killing many children.

In 1990, a young man who is angry with his girlfriend sets fire to the Happy Land Social Club in the Bronx. Eighty-seven people die.

One out of every four American households experiences a theft or a violent crime each year. In Detroit, in a two-month period in the summer of 1991, three hundred motorists were stopped at gunpoint and their cars taken. This new wave of crime, called "carjacking," increased the level of community fear in Detroit. A year later, in Washington, D.C., a young mother was forced from her car, became tangled in her seatbelt, and was dragged to her death. Her young child, still strapped into a carseat, was thrown out the window.

Murderous rage, it seems, is epidemic in our cities. During the week I have chronicled, St. Louis initiated a program in which citizens could turn in their guns—no questions asked—and receive fifty dollars. The guns would be melted down by the local police. Hundreds of guns were turned in the first few days. One woman told a police officer, "I bought it to kill my husband, but God took him before I could."

I would even suggest that something deeper than anger and rage is at work in this epidemic of crime. Over the past thirty years, we have seen more and more cases like Jeffrey Dahmer's, in which the criminals fit the profile of a sociopath. A simple definition of a sociopath is a criminal who is devoid of conscience—who feels no remorse for his acts and no pain for his victims.

I once had occasion to speak to the psychiatrist who treated the notorious murderer Charles Manson, who displayed marked sociopathic tendencies. "Is Manson crazy?" I asked the doctor. And she responded quickly, "Oh, no, he's not crazy; he's evil!"

This was not a theological discussion, but I understood her point. Even though sociopaths like Manson (or Jeffrey Dahmer) do not feel the pain of the victim or any remorse, they usually know clearly what they are doing.

There are, of course, some criminal offenders who are mentally ill. But the psychiatrist poses an intriguing question for our age. The mass killings, the savagery, the brutality, the maiming, the raping of the very young and the very old is far more symptomatic of evil than of insanity or just plain bad behavior.

What does all of this mean to us as Christians? Simply that we are called to make a difference in our violent, fear-ridden society. If Americans are not safe in their own homes or their own blocks, in a sense it doesn't matter whether tensions are subsiding in the

Middle East or whether Russia and America are reducing their nuclear arsenals. We who are called to be peacemakers cannot ignore the ongoing wars on our streets. We also cannot ignore our call to minister to the many casualties of those wars—victim and perpetrator alike.

People, Not Statistics

And that brings me to the second thing I realized from my week of observing crime. Usually, I am not even aware of crimes unless they are exceptional; I have come to accept a daily dose of crime stories in stride. Like many citizens, I have become desensitized to crime. As a result, I tend to think of crime victims as statistics rather than human beings. Josef Stalin emphasized the same human tendency when he once said, "A single death is a tragedy, a million deaths is a statistic."

Why did the killing of twenty-two people in Killeen, Texas make national headlines? The answer is simple: because twenty-two people died. If a madman had entered the cafeteria and killed one or two people, the killing would have only made local news.

This is part of the problem of how we view crime. It becomes newsworthy when the numbers mount. The greater the tragedy, the greater the disaster, the more it garners our attention.

But victims are not statistics. Victims are individual human beings connected to other people who also suffer loss. We forget that reality at our peril.

Seventy-one-year-old Al Gratia and his wife, Ursula, were not statistics. This couple had been married forty-eight years when they sat down in that Killeen cafeteria with their daughter, Suzanna. Before the meal was over, Suzanna would see them lying in a pool of blood.

Pat Carney and Nancy Stansbury were schoolteachers who were killed by the same gunman, George Hennard. Pat and Nancy are not statistics, either. They are human beings.

And remember, the family and friends of those who are cheated, robbed, raped, or murdered are victims also. They, too, suffer through lengthy court proceedings. They must cope with the loss of loved ones or with the stress of living with someone in great pain. Some of these suffer emotional wounds they will carry their entire lives. Certainly the little girl who saw her grandmother shot down in that Killeen cafeteria will be affected by that experience for a long time.

In jail and prison ministry we rightly show compassion for offenders. We rightly seek to take the message of Christ's forgiveness behind bars. But I have long been convinced that we are never to do this at the expense of ignoring victims of crime. We must have compassion for both the offender and the victim simultaneously. In fact, if we reach out to the offender and ignore the victim, we are sending a contradictory message. In many areas of our country, ministries are reaching out to prisoners in record numbers but the suffering of survivors and victims is often overlooked. The gospel compels us to reach out to hurting people.

Daniel Vasquez, the warden of San Quentin prison, recalls a proposal from a group who opposes capital punishment. They wanted to build a white cross of stones, one for each of the 278 condemned murderers on death row.

Vasquez responded, "It would be more appropriate to build a really large cross with one stone for each of their 600 victims."

I would suggest that another cross, a simple wooden one, has already been erected for both the perpetrators and the victims of crime in our society. We who follow the One who died on that cross are uniquely equipped to reach out to all those who are hurting—victims as well as prisoners. For we have as our model One who was sent not only "to preach deliverance to the captives" but also "to heal the brokenhearted" (Luke 4:18 KJV).

1

Survivor:
A Victim's Perspective

Susan Lee

In this chapter, Susan Lee discusses with riveting emotion her personal journey as a survivor of a brutal crime. As the victim of a rape, she presents us at once with the dilemma of whether she would ever be a whole and functioning person again. This is a good place for us to begin our discussion of criminal justice issues because, without the possibility of healing, the thousands of victims in our society remain fragmented and broken.

Before her rape, the author seemed to live a charmed life. She mixed the professional challenges of the business world with an avid interest in aerobics and dance. We also see a life in which God was a casual appendage. During the crime, we hear her poignant cries to God and her very real fears of death.

At the heart of Susan's testimony is the word forgiveness. *What can possibly persuade her to forgive such a violent criminal? It becomes clear from this chapter that, apart from grace, such forgiveness is almost an impossibility. We also see that Ms. Lee's eventual decision to begin a dance ministry among prisoners is part of her personal therapy and healing. The chapter leave us with the strong conviction that victims need our understanding, sensitivity, attention, and support.*

It has been said that a survivor is one who lives to tell the tale. We who survive speak for those who can no longer speak for themselves. This has been called the responsibility of memory.

I am a survivor. And my tale is a story for our times. In the last decade, the crime of rape increased fourfold. Among the victims of the eighties: the Massachusetts woman who was gang raped in a pool hall; the Central Park jogger who was raped and brutalized, and me.

Some survivors put their stories down on paper for all to share. My story, my testimony, would be titled, "How I Found God through Rape."

How It Happened

It all began on 1 December 1981. It was a typical day in my successful career—busy, fulfilling, stimulating. News of a cancelled business trip thrilled me because it meant I could spend the evening with my first love—dance.

Ah, yes! Work and dance. Daily I aspired to the Greek balance of a healthy mind and a healthy body.

The soul? The spirit? Love? Well, I was always better at work than love. And though I had always believed in God, I felt (as did many of my contemporaries) that religion was intellectual suicide. It didn't allow one to think; it hindered the creative process; it made "sheep" and followers out of people. I wanted no part of that!

So, safely encased in my smug self-reliance, I left the high-powered world of business for my dance class. It was one of the best yet. My body, disciplined and controlled, responded accurately to the cues and the challenging routines. So intense was my concentration that I didn't feel shin splints developing. But I felt them once class was over anyway, so I paused briefly to ask the teacher about treatment. Another woman had the same problem, and the three of us chatted about ice packs, dancers, and the pains of keeping in shape.

Without warning, our conversation was interrupted. Two men with sawed-off shotguns faced us squarely and ordered us down on the floor. We scrambled frantically only to be caught, beaten,

and shoved to the ground, all the while hearing invective and ob-
scenities that my sheltered life had thus far precluded.

Dear God, I prayed. *I'm going to die. Forgive me for my sins. I'm sorry
if I hurt you; I'm sorry for a selfish life. Please don't let it be too painful.
Just let them shoot me and get it over with.*

Lying face down, I felt the butt of his gun as he hit me over the
head. A gravelly voice ordered, "You get over there and take off
your clothes." Again I felt his gun because I didn't move.

*Oh, God, I'm going to be raped. Please, God, find help. If you loved me,
you wouldn't allow this to happen to me. I did nothing to deserve this.
God where are you?*

"Hurry up," he demanded. Again my face stung with pain as
he kicked me with his boot. I felt my teeth loosen.

God, help me, I can't get my jogging shoes off, and he keeps beating me.

Then it happened. I was raped—a fate worse than cancer,
worse than death. Rape! The actual word sounds ominous. At
the time, I wasn't worried about the psychological repercussions
because I was sure that he would shoot me when he was
through. Instead, he cut the wires off the teacher's tape recorder
and tied me, still naked, face down. The other women were not
raped, but they were tied up as well by both of our assailants. We
were held hostage for two hours. There was nothing left to do
but pray:

*My God, if you let me live through this, I will try to find you again. I
did love you once as a child, but somewhere along the way I got too busy,
too smart, too self-reliant. I thought I didn't need you. I thought that I
knew it all. Yet, here I am now, tied up like an animal. Me, with all my
college degrees and my successful career, bound like a dog. But, Lord, you
too were bound in ignominy—nailed even. You also suffered blows to the
face, and you were innocent. Lord, if you let me live, I will try to find you.
I will use my talents to honor you. After all, you gave them to me to use
for your glory. I know that now. I guess I always knew it. And if I live,
maybe someday I can forgive the rapist, the way you forgave the thief on
the cross.*

Again without warning, they left as quickly as they had come.
I don't know why. They took our money, our jewelry, our credit
cards, and my body. They broke all my teeth. They cut my bleeding hands with wires. But they gave me something too. They gave
me back something I had lost on the proverbial road from child-

hood to adulthood. They returned to me a faith in a Creator who will go to any lengths to reach a misguided, independent, stubborn member of his flock.

Life among the Victims

During my recovery, a friend gave me a prayer which I now read daily because it reflects my past and makes sense out of my experience: "I asked for power, that I might have the praise of men. I was given weakness that I might know the need of God."

I still suffer. Every time I go to the dentist to repair my broken teeth, I am reminded of that horrific night and the excruciating pain that followed. Every time I hear the news that a woman has been raped, I cry for her and for me. And yet, deep in my heart, I feel that this night of terror marked my beginning, not my demise.

H. G. Wells once said, "If a man does not have God, he begins at no beginning and he ends at no end." I now have God and God has me—perhaps his most rebellious sheep. I know I will never be the same after this tragedy—I will be better.

And no offense to the ancient Greeks, though I still pursue knowledge and a healthy physique, Jesus Christ is now the pillar of my life.

In a flash of light on the Damascus Road, the apostle Paul met his God. In a lightning-bolt experience, on the wooden floor of an aerobic dance studio, I met my Lord. And though that night marked my spiritual turning point, I still had to pick my broken teeth up off that dance floor and start my life all over again.

What followed was an eight-year odyssey—a spiritual, mental, and physical journey that took me places that I never dreamed I would go.

The first place it took me was to a police lineup to try to identify my assailants.

Lineups. They're not like you see on television, where one person views a line of alleged criminals. Instead, many victims are shuffled from one room to another. Then, huddled together, they watch as criminals, behind glass, are marched out on stage like movie stars.

I studied other crime victims at these lineups.

Some clutched their purses to their chests as if protecting an infant. One man repeatedly fingered his wallet and counted his money. An older woman nervously removed white gloves, revealing a missing finger on her left hand. In a robbery attempt she had been told to take the ring off. Years of marriage and a few extra pounds had rendered the ring stuck for life. To get the ring, the robber had cut her finger off.

They were the maimed, the tortured, the crime victims. And I was one of them.

After that, every day took its toll. I developed a constant tremor in my hand. Sleeping and eating became impossible. I was too terrified to put my trash out at night.

And then there was the voice. The voice that echoed incessantly and punctuated my every activity. While brushing my teeth, washing dishes, standing at the water cooler, driving my car, I heard it: *You get over there and take off your clothes.*

I couldn't get rid of that voice.

I found it difficult and sometimes impossible to swallow. I existed on liquids alone. I trembled uncontrollably. My mind felt blurry and foggy. My doctor's urging sent me to another place I had never dreamed I would go. To a hospital.

The Beginnings of Compassion

This hospital didn't fix broken bones or bind up bloody wounds. But it was for the broken—the broken of spirit, the broken of mind, those broken by life. It was for those who suffered from such ailments as post traumatic stress syndrome, as I did.

This hospitalization was my humbling. I had always prided myself on my brains and talent. I had always been a straight-A student, and I thought I was better than most people, especially the kind of people who were in here. I had figured that their problems were due to weaknesses, that they deserved their fate.

But now I was one of them. My pride was smashed. My arrogance was totally gone. Never again would I think I was better.

Never again would I hear the cackling of panhandlers, see the twitching of a bag lady, the trembling hands of an alcoholic, or the writhing of the addicted without feeling compassion. Because, you see, I became one of them during my hospital stay. And on days when I feel a little too self-important, the Lord reminds me of this time.

Prior to the rape, I had been the quintessential member of the "me" generation, a typical American lost in visions of perfection. And in this fanatical pursuit, I didn't see the need for compassion and sensitivity. They just got in my way.

It's been said that compassion is feeling your pain in my heart. That's what began to happen to me.

Anger—and Healing

When I left the hospital, I had made progress. My hands were steady. My walk was brisk. And I vowed I would never be a victim again. I was now entering another phase of rape recovery, the most prolonged and dangerous one—the anger phase.

To relieve the anger, I took five or six aerobics classes a day. One time I figured I had done a thousand jumping jacks in the course of a night. I knew it was excessive, and I knew that excess was a sin, but I couldn't stop. It was the only way to assuage the anger so I could sleep that night.

For the first thirty-six chapters of the Book of Job, God allows Job to rant and rave and to ask him why. I, too, was candid with God, and I cried out to him much like Job. But I did my battle with God on the dance floor. Nightly, as I sweated profusely and exercised myself into exhaustion, I would ask God why he allowed the rape to happen. Both the exercise and the questioning were cathartic, part of my healing process. I felt almost as if I was sweating out the pain. Slowly, I was recovering.

Then it happened—the nightmare of every dancer and athlete. While running for a bus, I tripped over a curb and fell. Excruciating pain shot through my ankle. I stayed away from aerobics for two weeks, but then I had to go back. My body was used to doing thirty-four hours a week; I couldn't stay away any longer. But after class, I noticed a swelling of my left ankle that wouldn't go away.

A doctor's visit confirmed my worst fears. He said I had torn all the ligaments in my ankle, that I needed an operation, that my dancing days were over.

I couldn't believe it. I went for a second opinion, then a third. Finally, I had seen eight doctors, and they all said the same thing: "You will never dance again."

Crippled by my ankle injury and devastated by the doctors' prognosis, I had given up any hope of recovery when a friend recommended another doctor. This one was a basketball player, a skier, a consummate athlete. He had studied in Switzerland and had operated on members of the Olympic ski team.

This doctor was different. Instantly we had the mutual respect and rapport of fellow athletes. He understood how important dance and aerobics were to me.

His prognosis was different, too. He said the operation would be painful, the recovery long, but there was a good chance that I could dance again.

I was sure that this doctor was sent from God. I felt totally safe in his hands. He was gentle, soft-spoken, compassionate, brilliant—and black. I had been brutalized by a black rapist, and now God in his wisdom was seeing to it that a talented black doctor would put me back together again.

After the operation, I was laid up for two months, on crutches for four, and in physical therapy for two years. Daily I prayed to God that if he gave me my foot back, I would try to find a way to use my love of dance for his glory.

A Ministry Out of Adversity

One day, while reading a passage from Corrie ten Boom's *The Hiding Place*, I was inspired. It was the passage where she described her sister, Betsy, who had converted one of her Nazi interrogators. Corrie wrote: "There she was the prisoner and her judge—the victim and her victimizer."

What forgiveness! I thought. Forgiveness hadn't been easy for me. I had realized in retrospect that my excessive aerobics was an attempt to escape a bitter reality. But only when I had come to the point of truly forgiving had my pain eased and my anger ceased.

Suddenly, it came to me. *Prison.* I could go into prison and work with criminals, not only to be sure that I had forgiven, but to tell them my story—how Jesus found me. I could bring them the message of the gospel and assure them that if I can change, anyone can.

Then I had another thought. I could teach them aerobic dance and use my classes as a platform for the gospel message. Dance, exercise, and aerobics were common interests I could share with inmates. I could make it fun and show them what it means to be a joyful Christian.

After two years of physical therapy, I got my doctor's final okay. I found some women from my church who wanted to join this new dance ministry. We got together every weekend, choreographing songs and rehearsing. We decided that our class would be an hour long. Forty-five minutes would be dedicated to aerobics, and the last fifteen minutes would be for prayer, sharing, and calls to salvation. We were connected with the outreach ministries of our church, and they prepared the inmates for our arrival.

Only one thing bothered me: What would we call ourselves? Then one day, during my morning devotions, I was reading Psalm 30—and it came to me. There it was in God's word—my story, what Jesus had done for me: "You have turned my sadness into a joyful dance" (v. 11).

And he had. Only a loving God could create a ministry out of adversity. And only a gracious God would allow me to serve him by doing what I loved best—dance!

2

Victim-Offender Reconciliation

Don Smarto

In this chapter, the editor uses the chilling story of a tragic crime as the background for an exploration of a justice system that perpetuates victims' pain and the Christian alternative of healing and reconciliation for victim and offender alike.

Phyllis Bosler, the wife of a murder victim, tells her story for the first time in this book. The reader will be captivated by how she resists hatred and expresses compassion for the offender.

The editor then goes on to challenge the underlying assumptions of our system of justice and show how the way we prosecute and punish crime often gets in the way of healing and reconciliation. In particular, he explores the role of popular culture, including movies and television, in perpetuating myths about "good guys" and "bad guys" that have confused both our ethics and morality and influenced our treatment of offenders and victims.

The editor ends the chapter with a personal call to the church to be agents of healing and reconciliation in an often heartless and impersonal system. He musters both biblical examples and practical suggestions to show how the church can involve itself in reforming the system, presenting alternative forms of justice, and ministering to those who have been hurt both by crime and by the system.

It was four days before Phyllis could return to her house. She had had many happy times in the parsonage, but now the sounds of laughter and music were conspicuously absent as she entered. It was Christmas Day, and the walls were black from the charcoal used to lift fingerprints. "The house seemed dark and very cold," Phyllis remembers. "The detectives had cleaned up the blood, but I still found it everywhere, splattered on doors, behind appliances." Then she came to the spot where her husband had been murdered. "I would let no one step on it." She covered it gently with a small rug. In her own way, it became a memorial.

Phyllis Bosler is a woman of great courage and sensitivity who endured the tragic and senseless murder of her husband. Phyllis's daughter, Suzanne, is a victim/survivor who was left for dead by her father's murderer.

This is the dramatic story of the survivors of a brutal crime.

The Story of a Crime

Phyllis and Bill Bosler had been married twenty-nine years. Bill had been pastor of Peace Church in Miami for eight years. The Boslers and their daughter lived in the parsonage adjacent to the church.

"The church people loved Bill," Phyllis says. Coming out of a tradition of the Church of the Brethren and the Mennonite church, these were people who did not believe in the death penalty, revenge, or retaliation. They were in every way peaceful people who loved Jesus Christ.

Several days before Christmas, the Bosler home was decorated with a Christmas tree, lights, wrapped gifts under the tree, and an array of colorful Christmas cards on the table. The homes of Bill's congregation were also decorated with strings of multicolored Christmas lights.

It was 22 December 1986. Phyllis had traveled from Florida to Indiana to be with another daughter who had recently given Phyllis and Bill a grandchild. That afternoon at 2:30 P.M. she was Christmas shopping at a mall near her daughter's house.

At the same hour, at the parsonage, Bill was calmly reading in the living room. Suzanne was taking a shower.

There was a knock on the door. It was James Campbell, age nineteen, who lived about five blocks away from the church with his aunt. He did not know Pastor Bosler. As the prosecution later reconstructed the events, he probably picked the house at random.

Bill Bosler opened the door. There was no witness to any conversation, so nothing is known of what transpired verbally. What is known is that James Campbell had a large butcher knife concealed up his sleeve. He pulled it out and began to slash savagely at Bill, cutting him deeply on his hands and arms.

According to the investigating homicide detectives, the pastor staggered backward, bracing himself in a doorway, stunned and in shock. His bloody handprints were found on the doorposts.

Suzanne had now emerged from the shower. The noises seemed unusual to her. As she opened her bedroom door, she was horrified to see the cold-blooded assailant stab her father in the chest and then in the right ear. She ran out in an impulsive and desperate attempt to save her father. At this point, Campbell turned on Suzanne and stabbed her three times. She fell to the floor. He stabbed her again on the right side of the head, the butcher knife going four to five inches into her brain, yet she remained conscious, her eyes open to the horrible scene. The pastor was still alive too, on his hands and knees. Campbell turned around and stabbed him savagely in the back.

Phyllis's other daughter suddenly had a strange premonition during the shopping. Abruptly she said to her mother, "I don't want to shop anymore. Let's go home immediately." Phyllis thought this odd, but they did return home while the attack continued thousands of miles away.

Suzanne remembers watching red blood soak her white robe. She was lying on her stomach. Several times the truculent intruder touched her back to see if she was breathing. She remembers trying to hold perfectly still, knowing that if he thought she was alive, he would continue to stab her. Campbell went through the house, ransacking it. He changed into one of Bill's blue suits, planning to throw out his own blood-soaked clothes. He was in the house for another twenty minutes. Three or four times he returned to feel Suzanne, who held her breath, desperately trying not to move or make a sound. He lifted her robe but did not rape her.

Campbell then left the house abruptly. Suzanne was able to crawl to a phone. The first time she dialed incorrectly. When she did manage to dial 911, a young woman who answered did not understand the seriousness of the situation. Part of Suzanne's skull was imbedded in her brain, and she could feel the blood covering her face and body. "Just stay calm," the 911 dispatcher said, "we'll have help on the way." Suzanne, who ordinarily never got angry, shouted some expletives. But soon she heard sirens, then someone banging on the door. Campbell had slammed the front door after him, locking it. An officer went from door to door trying to find a way in. He was about to break open a glass back door when he saw Suzanne's bloodied hand reach up and unlatch it. The officer felt Bill's neck. He was dead at the scene. Suzanne was soon in surgery.

The Bad News Spreads

It was 7:00 P.M. in the Indiana home of Phyllis's other daughter. Phyllis answered the phone. "This is a detective," the voice said, "from Miami. I need the phone number of your son-in-law. Phyllis gave the number, hung up, and then immediately prayed. She feared that her son-in-law was in trouble, and she told her daughter. The daughter speculated that it could have been an old ticket or a problem with a title transfer of a car. Phyllis never suspected the news was for her.

By now, the parsonage was swarming with detectives and crime-scene investigators. They put black charcoal on the walls to lift prints. They took photographs of Bill's hacked-up body, which was then transported to the county morgue. In the meantime, Suzanne fought for life.

Phyllis's son-in-law had received the detective's phone call at work and promptly returned home. Phyllis remembers, "I was concerned about my son-in-law, fearing that he was in trouble."

The young man appeared nervous and trembling. "Let's go into the kitchen," he pleaded. "I've got something very difficult to tell you." Again, Phyllis was concerned about him. "Let's please hold hands," he urged. The words came out fast: "Bill's been murdered!" Phyllis put her head down and covered her face with her hands. As if in a vision, she saw her husband's body lying on the floor in the exact position detectives would later confirm, although her son-in-law had not described the manner of death. She would not learn of her daughter Suzanne for another hour.

By now the electrifying news had circulated throughout Bill's church like lightning. Church members turned off all their Christmas lights in a symbolic gesture. They would never turn them on again throughout the entire 1986 Christmas season. They were stunned and shocked by the murder of the pastor they loved. So often he had preached about heaven; now he was there.

Once she heard the news, Phyllis remembers, "It was like a shot of novocaine. Everything went numb, everything stopped inside me." The family took an early morning flight to Atlanta, with a changeover to Miami. At the airport, a policewoman friend picked them up. She used excessive profanity to describe her reaction to what had happened. She was more outraged than Phyllis at the tragic proportions of the crime.

A detective advised Phyllis against viewing her husband's body. A member of the church went to the morgue for identification. Bill Bosler's mangled body was entirely covered with a sheet except for a part of his face.

Suzanne was now in intensive care, and the brain surgeon informed Phyllis: "It took four hours just to get out every fragment of bone and skull that was imbedded in her brain. We had to remove a lot of brain tissue." The surgeon sounded pessimistic, but Phyllis believed in the power of God and refused to give up hope.

On Christmas Eve, Phyllis was sitting with a detective at the hospital. "Did he suffer?" she asked the detective. He seemed uneasy with the question. He almost whispered, "Not long."

Phyllis never saw her husband's body. In accordance with his wishes (and their church practice), there was no visitation or funeral. The body was cremated and the ashes spread over the waters of the Gulf of Mexico.

Gradually Suzanne began to recover. Half of her head was shaven. Fifty large stitches held her together. Miraculously, however, she had no loss of vision or hearing. Phyllis had feared that her daughter would be a "vegetable," but by God's power, she was improving physically. Suzanne was also in therapy for her emotional wounds. She went through months of hysterical crying, remembering the incident, and feeling great guilt that she did not save her father. Eventually Suzanne returned to her job as a beautician, but she would never forget, never be the same.

Phyllis never moved back into the once-happy parsonage. It took her nearly a year to remove her possessions. The house seemed cold and dark to her every time she entered it. She only showed the slightest anger when anyone stepped on "the spot."

Campbell was arrested after a few days. During the trial it was revealed that he had been released from prison after a short time for a previous murder. He was mentally unstable but was sedated during the trial so he would remain calm. The jury found him guilty of first-degree murder, first-degree with premeditation, and several other counts. Campbell is now on death row in Florida.

Five Years Later

How does Phyllis survive five years later? "I just take one day at a time," she says. She has repeatedly declined interviews with Geraldo Rivera, Oprah Winfrey, Phil Donahue, and other talk show hosts, saying, "I'm not ready for that. I don't want a movie made out of this either. Bill was a loving person, a good father and husband. He was a pastor who was knowledgeable and caring. That's how I want him remembered—not as a victim, but as a person.

"I do not hate my husband's murderer," she adds. "I feel sorry for him." She is convinced that he should not be released from prison—"I never want this to happen to another family." And she has not been able to visit him in prison. But she has always been able to see James Campbell as a person and to have great concern for him. She also sees the futility of taking another life through exercising the death penalty. Killing Campbell, she believes, will not help her emotionally or bring back wholeness to her family. If anything, she believes Campbell's execution would only intensify her pain and that of her family.

Today Phyllis is involved in prison ministry. She has a deep desire to let other murderers know that there is forgiveness both from God and victims. She speaks with authority, as someone who has survived great tragedy. She also has become sensitized to other issues, such as abortion: "I feel that the killing of an unborn child is just as much murder as what Campbell did to my husband."

Sadly, Phyllis's stance of mercy for her husband's killer has brought its own share of pain. "I am a victim in two ways," she declares. "I am the victim of my husband's murder and daughter's attempted murder. And I am the victim of other people's harsh judgment." This included a pastor who, knowing that Phyllis and her husband oppose the death penalty, said to her repeatedly, "Campbell should fry!"

Is she angry at God? "No," she responds quickly, "this was clearly man's sin." And for victims she has this advice, "It is important to get over the anger and the hatred. It only turns you on yourself. I've met many parents whose children have been murdered and who are consumed with hatred and a wish for revenge. They need to get beyond that."

That doesn't mean, however, that the pain of being a victim is over for Phyllis. It is clear as she recounts the story, as she fights back tears, that the painful reality is just beneath the surface. Nevertheless, Phyllis has grown through her grief and grasped on to hope. "I still have pain and scars," she proclaims, "but I know I will see my husband again."

No Place for Healing

At the heart of God's call for justice is the concept of righteousness. And this reaches far beyond the simple idea of punishment of crimes and redress for injustices. Wherever possible, we should try to achieve healing both for individuals and society. We should work to mend broken relationships—and there is truly no greater example of a shattered relationship than in the case of a criminal and his or her victim. More often than not, unfortunately, our criminal justice system works against mending relationships and healing for either the victim, the criminal, or society at large.

For instance, there is no place for the victim in today's courtrooms. Only if they have important information to contribute or can act as eyewitnesses will victims be called upon to testify.

Phyllis Bosler, who was not present at the time of the crime and did not know the assailant, was told clearly by prosecutors that her role was to make no comments to the press, not to contact the assailant's family—essentially, to be mute. The prosecutors were especially concerned that she not express any convictions regarding mercy for the killer. (No doubt there are many prosecutors who care deeply about victims, but I have also met many who simply use them to play on the jurors' sympathies and help them win cases.)

Our criminal justice system also makes little room for restitution or reconciliation. Criminals are rarely given the opportunity to make up for what they have done by returning money to the victim, cleaning up damage, or helping out in other ways. Instead, they are typically punished with fines or prison sentences that do little for the victims except possibly feed a sense of revenge.

And I am convinced our problems go even deeper than leaving out a formal role for the victim and omitting any chance for reconciliation and restitution. At the root of our problems, I believe, is the adversarial nature of our court system.

We know from watching the volatile eruptions on *L.A. Law* or the dramatic cross-examinations on *Perry Mason* reruns that our courts are based on the idea of pitting one lawyer against another. The roots of this adversary system lie in early centuries, when contests were used to settle differences. In medieval jousts, for example, two knights charged one another on horses to determine a winner. In the seventeenth and eighteenth centuries, dueling was considered an acceptable way to resolve disputes. The concept of the "Wild West" gunfight was simply an extension of dueling.

One clear principle of the adversary system is that there has to be a winner and a loser. That remains at the heart of our justice system today.

The concept of a contest in which someone clearly wins and someone else loses is ingrained in us at a very early age in our society. Children in Little League quickly learn about winners and losers, especially from vocal parents on the sidelines. And although sportsmanship is emphasized in both high school and college sports, coaches who don't produce winning seasons are soon replaced. The message to children is not subtle.

In professional sports, of course, winning is the name of the game. The very existence of a Super Bowl or a World Series assumes that there is one purpose, one overall goal in any endeavor: to be the best. That there will be losers is a foregone conclusion.

In the courtroom we see a more civilized contest, in which guns and muscles are replaced by articulate tongues. The battle is fought out between the prosecutor and the defense attorney using evidence, witnesses, logic, and convincing arguments as ammunition. The defendant is proved either innocent or guilty. One lawyer wins. One lawyer loses.

During my years of working in the criminal justice system, I sat through hundreds of hours of courtroom testimony and observed quite a few lengthy trials. In many, I perceived a type of unspoken morality drama being played out. When the prosecutor won, it was a triumph of good over evil. Those who violated the law, the criminals, were the bad people. Those who proved their guilt and vindicated the victim with a penalty such as incarceration were the shining knights.

The problem with this system is that there is rarely room for healing. The victim is kept apart from the offender and, in many cases, the prosecutor fuels the anger of the victim or the victim's family. There is no formal role for reconciliation between victim and offender, no opportunity for mediation or mutually agreed restitution. People are kept apart, not brought closer together.

Good Guys and Bad Guys

What is our emotional investment in adversarial justice? Concepts have been ingrained in us during our formative years. The game of "cops and robbers" is a type of childhood morality play. Those who grew up in the forties and fifties had movie serials and television westerns as a model: General Custer and the cavalry were the good guys and the Indians and outlaws were the bad guys. (The Lone Ranger, whose sidekick was a Native American, presented a dilemma.) Later with the television show, *The Untouchables,* the G-men and Elliott Ness were the good guys and the gangsters were the bad guys.

These were simple games. Beyond childhood exuberance and the expenditure of energy, there was a simple goal: the good guys were to prevail, and the bad guys were to get caught, locked up, or killed. But these simple and easy to understand rules just don't apply in real life. For one thing, the great majority of offenders don't go away. More than 94 percent will return to the community—only more hostile, more violent, more educated in sophisticated criminal ways.

But on a more basic level, this "good" and "bad" distinction tends to ignore the common humanity of both "guys"—and this easily leads to pride on one side or cynical hopelessness on the other. From a biblical concept we are all—"good" and "bad," winner and loser, victim and perpetrator, defense and prosecution—sinners in need of grace. We have *all* sinned and fall short of the glory of God. The danger of good-bad, win-lose thinking is that it ignores this basic fact about all of us and blocks the possibility of both healing and redemption.

Yet another wrinkle in this "good" and "bad" picture is that it's not always easy to tell who the good guy is. Many minority children in urban settings, for example, have learned to distrust authority figures. The videotaped beating of a black man by Los Angeles police which was repeatedly shown on American television made it difficult for many to distinguish who the bad guys really were.

In addition, our culture, especially our movies, have turned many criminals into folk heroes. The *Godfather* saga, for example, presented organized crime figures as attractive and even admirable. Ruthless heroes like Billy the Kid, who shot almost all his victims in the back, have been the subject of films and even a major ballet. Kids in the "cops and robbers" game who once would only want to play an FBI man now might find John Dillinger, Clyde Barrow, or Al Capone more attractive.

At the same time, many of our popular portrayals of "good" send a message that you can break the law for a higher purpose or if you can get away with it. Take the 1971 Clint Eastwood film, *Dirty Harry*. With the famous line, "Go ahead; make my day," the cop convinces a villain to reach for his gun, then shoots him in "self-defense." Because the bad guy had been released on a technicality, the film assumes, Eastwood's character was justified in killing him.

Two other films, *Serpico* (1973) and *Prince of the City* (1981)—each supposedly based on fact-are about police officers who stood up to internal corruption. In *Prince of the City*, the prosecutors are made to appear as the bad guys who push the cop or expose police corruption. The main character says, "I wanted to do something to show I was a good guy, not a bad guy." *Serpico* is about a New York detective who is unwilling to take bribes. He says, "I feel like a criminal because I don't take money." Both films appear to demonstrate that the honest cop loses the loyalty of his peer group and is dubbed a traitor.

A similar message is sent by more recent films starring Sylvester Stallone and Arnold Schwarzenegger. Stallone's *Cobra* and Schwarzenegger's *Raw Deal* (both 1986) send the message that it is okay to kill the bad guys on the street because they are too influential to get to court and, if they do get to court, they will only receive a light punishment. These films and others like them are extremely violent. They feature weapons of extreme force used with great passion—and bloody results.

I believe these films represent a cathartic acting out of the public's general discontent with our ability to wage effective war on crime. They also demonstrate the breakdown of clear lines of morality: people in authority are seen as corrupt or as having to resort to the same methods as criminals in order to succeed. Most important, I believe they illustrate the ultimate futility in our adversarial approach to justice.

Rethinking the System

What then would be a solution to this mixed-up, painful, and potentially dangerous situation? An obvious beginning point is reform of the system. I believe that as a society we need to rethink the way we conduct our courts and impose our consequences on people who break the law.

An important first step is to ensure equality before the law for all people. We must not tolerate authority figures, especially frontline police, who practice racial prejudice, abuse the rights of those arrested, or commit crimes in the name of justice.

Second, we must vigorously prosecute those who subvert justice by means of bribes, "deals," and special favors. Judges, police officers, attorneys, organized crime figures, or any others who manipulate the system to their own ends do as much harm in the long term as thieves and drug peddlers.

Third, we must find a way to return to the practice of swift and certain punishment. The endless delays, pointless motions for continuance, and ongoing appeals not only cost the taxpayer; they also blunt the effect of the punishment and draw out the victim's ordeal. The months or even years it takes to conclude a serious trial today could be used in other, more healing ways.

If an offense is serious enough to require three years in prison, then the offender should serve three years. Any "time off for good behavior" should be shaved from the basic sentence only. At present, most criminals can calculate how much time they really will serve if they keep their noses clean in prison. With the massive overcrowding in prisons even violent offenders will usually serve only half of their sentence, and with the federal court orders restricting prison populations, some violent offenders are being released through the back door at an alarming rate.

Increasing the swiftness and certainty of consequences for crime will, of course, require some changes—both in the law and in the ways our criminal justice system is structured. This leads to my fourth conclusion. I believe prisons must be used as a scarce resource for those who are violent and who present a clear danger to society. There are many better ways to penalize and send a strong message to nonviolent offenders—including confiscation of wealth, community service, home custody, and negotiated restitution.

The American people are waking up to the reality that prisons are a nonsolution. The incredible cost of building and maintaining these facilities is burdensome—millions of dollars per facility. Without a change in that trend, we are passing this economic burden on to our grandchildren.

More important, we are waking up to the fact that, more often than not, prisons just don't change people. More often, offenders emerge from their sentences with a graduate degree in crime and an added dose of rage against society.

The fact is: Buildings have never changed people or touched the human heart. That is why the so-called rehabilitation theories over the years in corrections institutions have failed. If we really want to change our criminal justice system for the better, we need to look seriously at some alternatives.

A System without a Heart

I am convinced that, without reform, our criminal justice system tends to perpetuate a crime victim's pain rather than working toward healing. But as I have indicated, the problem goes deeper than procedures. Simply put, the adversarial system lacks heart. In fact, the way we deal with victims and offenders alike lacks heart at every level—from the police officers walking their beat to the hospital personnel who receive the victims of crime to the newspaper journalists, and TV reporters and the prosecutors and judges. And I base that conclusion not only on observation, but on my own painful experience.

Two years ago I was preaching at San Quentin prison and spent most of the afternoon with a hundred inmates, the great majority of whom had committed murder. I felt safe.

At the end of the day, I left the prison and was walking down a well-traveled street in San Francisco. A young man approached me. I thought he was going to ask for directions, so I stopped to help him. He demanded all my money, and when I resisted he punched me in the face, breaking my nose.

I was certainly angry at him for several days, but then my anger melted into both empathy and compassion for him. He was obviously a troubled young man. Whether the reason for his violence was related to drugs, mental illness, or the way he was raised, I have remembered to pray for him frequently.

But the worst part of my experience was not the actual assault and battery, but the emotional assault I suffered from an uncaring public and a depersonalizing system.

Three people stood waiting at a bus stop only feet away from where I was attacked. As I lay on the ground, bruised and bleeding, they all pretended to look in other directions. Not one of them attempted to help me.

Over the years I have watched too many James Bond movies. I had come to believe that individuals can take thirty or forty punches and still be coherent. I must confess not only that one solid punch was sufficient to give me a momentary blackout, but also that the resulting pain almost immobilized me. My eyes were tearing, my nose was bleeding, I had dirt on my arms and the side of my face. I staggered across the street to a hotel parking garage and saw a parking attendant in a glass booth. As I approached him with a plea to call the police, he shut his door and his window and motioned for me to go away.

When I did call the police from a phone booth, the kind dispatcher told me that a police car would be there promptly. For half an hour I sat on a curb, waiting. Whenever someone approached, I felt near panic, thinking the assailant had returned. Even shadows made me jumpy. When no police car arrived, I noticed a police car sitting in front of a fast-food restaurant. Holding my face, I walked in, and the officers immediately took me out of the view of the patrons and into the parking lot. When I explained what had happened, one police officer, indignant over his disturbed dinner break, said, "Well, what do you want us to do about it?" The officers tried to convince me to let the matter go. They explained that I was from another city, that my assailant was probably a drifter who would never be caught, and if he was, nothing would happen to him.

Through persistence, I convinced the officers to take me in their car to look for my assailant. Now came yet another indignity. As I sat in the back of the police car, holding my swollen nose and bloodstained face, I realized that passersby were looking at me as if I had been arrested. Forty minutes later, we were still circling the same block. I was confident that the assailant was smart enough not to stay in the vicinity of the crime. At no time did the police officers show any compassion, understanding, or sympathy. In fact, they did not even offer to drive me to a hospital. I drove myself to a hospital, and I found that the nurses, emergency room doctor, and other personnel referred to me as the "broken nose in trauma room three." An X-ray technician, in the process of taking pictures of my neck, pulled my head and created excessive pain. When I complained, he scolded me like a child and said "We'll have to be here all night if you don't cooperate."

Of course, waiting is a big part of hospitalization. It took me almost six and a half hours before I was released at two in the morning. When I returned home, the victim of a violent crime, the real emotional and psychological injury had not come from the offender, but from the police, the medical personnel, and especially the three individuals at the bus stop and the man in the parking garage who failed to help.

My trauma was very small compared to what Phyllis and Suzanne Bosler experienced, but I know in a small way that being a victim can leave lasting scars—and that many of the scars are souvenirs of a heartless and impersonal system.

The Church with Heart

In a fallen world, a world seething with anger and hatred, it should not be surprising that our criminal justice system is often an agent of pain rather than healing for victims. Reform is an important first step. Humanizing the system as much as possible is absolutely necessary. And I believe the church should be actively involved in both these steps. Being salt and light in our society must include lobbying for a system that is more humane for all involved and more conducive to real justice.

In particular, the church can be instrumental in helping provide alternatives to the typical "win-lose" court battle. The biblically rooted practice of restitution offers the possibility of reconciliation rather than revenge. Its purpose is to make the victim whole in terms of a return of money or property and to be therapeutic for the offender as well.

Several years ago I went through eight hours of training in V.O.R.P.—Victim Offender Reconciliation Program. This program, which came out of the Mennonite church, has been used in Kitchener, Ontario, Canada, and Elkhart, Indiana. Similar programs, like the Neighborhood Justice Center of Atlanta, are being used successfully elsewhere. The concept is simple and biblical. Responsible members of the community volunteer their time and are trained to sit down with victim and offender to agree upon a mutually acceptable restitution and to reconcile relationships.

The V.O.R.P. model would not have worked for the Bosler family. Bringing together violent offenders and their victims typically creates too much stress and psychological trauma. Crimes such as murder, rape, and child abuse are best handled by the courts. But "white collar" crimes such as embezzlement and forgery provide fertile opportunity for community mediation. Property crimes such as vandalism, trespassing, criminal damage to property, theft, and burglary can also be mediated by volunteer citizens. And church members steeped in the Bible's sense of justice and reconciliation would make excellent mediators.

In addition to facilitating the healing of relationships, mediation benefits the public in another way. Courtroom congestion and case backlog has reached crisis proportions in many cities. Victim-offender reconciliation programs can help relieve the logjam by removing cases from the system. Such a program can be used as a condition of probation, a prerelease contract, or an alternative to a courtroom trial. This would translate into tremendous savings for the taxpayer.

What are the consequences for the offender's failure to abide by the agreement? The deterrent here is obvious. If the offender is not sincere about the restitution and reconciliation, he or she proceeds to court and whatever sentence the judge hands down.

In addition, I believe the church can play a vital role in giving heart to the system by ministering directly to those who may be victims of an impersonal system as well as victims of a crime.

I believe the parable of the Good Samaritan in Luke 10:30–37 gives us a good example of the role the church is called to play. Christ told this story to an expert on Moses' laws, and he made it very clear that the priest and the temple assistant who did not stop to aid the robbery victim because they were busy with religious duties were not the heroes of the story. It was an unlikely individual, a member of a hated foreign race, who showed compassion by stopping, binding the victim's wounds, bringing him to an inn, and paying the innkeeper for his care. The Good Samaritan put aside racial feelings, social status, and cultural bias to help the victim. He saw the hurt man as a person and loved him by helping him.

And that, as I see it, is the church's role in bringing about righteousness. We can be informed about our criminal justice system. We can lobby for reform. We certainly need to be involved in programs of restitution and reconciliation. But we also need to be actively involved in "binding up" victims' wounds—offering physical aid when necessary, reaching out to comfort them in their loss, standing by them during the long, often-dehumanizing court process, praying for their healing, helping them learn to forgive and move on.

I even believe churches should have a victim fund (like a deacon's fund) that is earmarked for the needs of victims. As in the Good Samaritan parable, the victim does not need to be a member of their church or even known. How can the church identify local victims? Here the answer is easy. The daily newspaper tells us about crimes and about victims.

What a dynamic way for the church to minister! In the case of a rape victim, the church's victim fund could assist in paying for psychiatric or psychological counseling. When a child is killed, the church's victim fund can assist with funeral expenses and pay for babysitting children while the parents attend court. Even smaller crimes have victims who can be helped. Imagine your church's youth group helping to remove graffiti from the side of an elderly person's home or garage. Imagine the deacons of your church replacing a window shattered by vandals. The fund could even be used to replace essential items lost in a burglary.

I do not believe the victims have to be believers to receive our help and compassion. In fact, what better way to demonstrate that the church is truly the body of Christ than by bringing hope and healing to those who are victims of crime.

Part 2

Punishing
with Compassion

Introduction

Months after mass-serial killer Ted Bundy was executed, I was sitting in his cell. I knew about his crimes. I had seen him speak on television, but he remained an enigma to me. I sat on his bed. I looked at his sink and toilet fixture and the small adjoining cell where he had kept the law books he used when he had acted as his own defense attorney. Bundy was a former law student. He was intelligent and good looking. He had been involved in social activity, including political campaigns in the northwestern United States.

So the question I asked myself that day was: Who was Ted Bundy? Was he evil? Could he have changed? Was he so far gone that killing him was society's only recourse?

I felt no eerie sensations sitting in Bundy's cell until I stood up and looked directly in his mirror, a highly polished sheet of metal bolted to the wall. I thought to myself, *The man who saw his face in this mirror every day for several years is now dead.* Yet, according to the Bible, he was still created in the image of God. He was still a person. Even though he had done terrible things, it is possible that God forgave him if he had truly repented in his heart. I am at a loss to understand Christians who celebrate the death penalty. "An eye for an eye, a tooth for a tooth" is proclaimed as a right. I am perplexed when people quote the Old Testament without any reference to the New Testament. Jesus clearly said that we do not have to do something just because we have a legal right to do it. The woman caught in adultery and thrown at his feet could have been stoned to death, but Jesus showed mercy. Repeatedly,

Jesus talks about forgiveness, walking the extra mile, turning the other cheek, surrendering our cloak, not having a spirit of retaliation, revenge, or vengeance. We are specifically commanded to love our enemies.

As Ted Bundy's execution date drew closer, John Tanner spent more and more time with him in a Bible study. John Tanner was a local prosecutor who believed that everyone, including Bundy, was entitled to the opportunity of an individual choice to turn away from sin and follow God. According to Tanner, Bundy made a commitment to Christ the night before his execution. Many believed this was a manipulative ploy. And yet, though I cannot answer the question of whether Bundy is saved, I don't think anyone can say that he is not.

On the day of Bundy's execution, on the property of the prison, vendors were selling trinkets (including miniature electric chairs on key chains) and refreshments. An atmosphere of festivity prevailed. There were chants of "fry baby, fry!" One newspaper quoted state Senator Harry Johnston as proclaiming that Governor Graham had signed a contract with the Tennessee Valley Authority to receive more electricity for Bundy, which proved to be false. The day after his execution, one weekly magazine reported, "Bundy was executed yesterday, but he immediately filed an appeal." In addition to the tasteless humor was the hate mail that John Tanner received. One person said, "It's too late for someone like Bundy to turn to God on the eve of his execution." I must assume the writer did not know that one of the thieves hanging beside the crucified Jesus had a change of heart and that Jesus immediately extended mercy and compassion to him when he said, "I tell you the truth, today you will be with me in paradise" (Luke 23:43).

I believe the execution of Bundy brings a sharp clarity to the issue of punishing with compassion. He is one of this century's most infamous criminals. I am not debating whether it was right or wrong to execute him. I am suggesting, however, that the passing of any life is a solemn event—not an occasion for celebration.

Statistically we have not been able to prove that accelerating the use of the death penalty reduces crime. There are many who still believe it does. Of course, a 1991 poll in *U.S. News & World Re-*

port revealed that 20 percent of adults in the United States still think the sun goes around the earth and 45 percent believe dinosaurs and humans lived at the same time. The fact that large numbers of people believe something does not make it so.

What Is Appropriate Punishment?

The key question articulated some years ago by Chuck Colson was not whether or not we punish people, but *how* we punish people—what is the *appropriate* punishment? Can we punish in such a way as not to devastate the offender's life and preclude any possibility of change, rehabilitation, and restoration?

The first prison in America was Newgate Prison in Connecticut. It was used for prisoners of the Revolutionary War. In August 1991, I visited the solitary confinement area of that prison—an abandoned sulfur mine. I had to practically crawl forty feet underground until I got to the small cell. The brackets men were chained to were still in the stone. The cell was dark and cold. Water ran down the walls. The ceiling was so low I could not stand erect.

It is interesting to note that, although Newgate stayed in operation for more than a hundred years, it was considered a modern prison that was humane and compassionate. As a punishment, they would tie up a prisoner and give him a hundred lashes with a whip. During that same period, Navy rules aboard ships allowed a thousand lashes. Newgate, therefore, was seen as a compassionate institution.

This illustrates that our sense of justice and compassion is often relative. We compare ourselves to other societies. In America, for example, we often point out that we do not mutilate people for crimes, as they do in many countries of the Middle East. We do not chop off the hand of someone who steals. And yet a young man imprisoned for the same crime in an American prison can easily be the victim of a violent gang rape. (There are indications that more than 50 percent of male inmates are raped during the first thirty days of confinement.) As a result of this physically painful and humiliating crime against him, he can also contract AIDS. In effect, he may be given a death sentence for a nonviolent offense such as forging a check. It is simply not compassionate treatment to have prisoners become victims of crimes worse than the crimes that sent them to prison.

Public opinion says, "They deserve what they get." A "lock them up and throw away the key" mentality still prevails in our country. And such thinking often has little relevance to whether the punishment is effective or appropriate—much less whether it leads to reconciliation for victim, offender, and the society at large. The principle of compassionate punishment helps us overcome that mindset and move on toward corrections that promote both justice and healing.

Having laid that foundation, let's look briefly at some of the forms of punishment that have been proposed as alternatives to incarceration and examine their feasibility and effectiveness.

Is Probation a Good Alternative to Incarceration?

Probation is probably the most widely used alternative to incarceration in our criminal justice system. It is meant to be a form of supervision under court restrictions that prevents a convicted person from going to already overcrowded jails or prisons. As such, it is a potentially useful and compassionate corrections alternative. Unfortunately, probation as it is used across America, especially in large cities, is often a farce, because there are simply not enough officers to supervise probationers adequately.

It is vital that the probation officer have sufficient time with the probationer to monitor employment and family status and to engage in counseling that gets to the underlying feelings and frustrations of the individual. But with a probation system that is responsible for more than a million people nationwide—and with typical caseloads of more than a hundred probationers—the system degenerates into a check-in, check-out process. Offenders can easily manipulate the system and the officers by telling them what they want to hear.

As a society, we simply have to put more money into hiring professional probation officers, as opposed to more prison cells. If these officers handled an average caseload of twenty cases, they could meet with each individual for forty-five minutes a week or more. This would provide the structure and supervision that might really help stabilize the offender. Unless this happens, the probation system is simply not a workable alternative.

Can Intensive Supervision Reduce Prison Overcrowding?

Many cities are using intensive supervision as an alternative to imprisonment. Caseloads under thirty make excellent supervision possible; however, with the state of our economy and cutbacks in government spending, the use of intensive supervision has been restricted.

Shock probation, called that because visits are more frequent and the supervision more intense, is another form of intensive supervision. The judge may combine forms of periodic imprisonment, such as work release, with other requirements such as drug and alcohol counseling, meeting with a psychologist, actively seeking employment, and continuing education. This puts the burden on the offenders. If they want to avoid jail or prison, they will live up to the requirements. If they are not willing to work, increase job skills, or further their education, then the next phase of punishment is acceptable.

Can Boot Camp Deter Crime?

"Boot camp" is another alternative to traditional incarceration that has been tried in some states. This controversial model involves taking offenders who otherwise would be going to jail and putting them in a highly structured environment for fifty or sixty days. This program, modeled on a Marine Corps boot camp, is based on extreme discipline. It features exercises, work details, drills and marching, and militaristic officers shouting commands at every turn. It also uses extreme peer pressure to mold the individual's behavior.

These concepts are not new to corrections, of course. During the seventies, many case workers practiced the positive peer model by putting juvenile delinquents in residential treatment centers where stronger youth helped the younger ones conform to acceptable behavior. And the basic concept of behavior modification through rewards and punishments has long been used in prisons. In Russia, for example, some prisons that have two food lines, one with acceptable food and one with substandard fare. It does not take a clinical psychologist to analyze that people prefer rewards over punishments and will modify their behavior to receive the reward.

But the key question both with positive peer culture or the intense reward-punishment approach of a boot camp is: Will the changes last? The evidence, unfortunately, suggests otherwise. On 13 November 1991, ABC television news devoted a segment to the boot camp philosophy and a study of existing models. Unfortunately, the story demonstrated that, although many of the men attending boot camp made initial progress, they lapsed back into crime when they returned to their original neighborhoods, drug contacts, and dysfunctional homes. The future of this method is still under study and review.

The problem with boot camp is that, like older correctional philosophies such as lock step, hard labor, and solitary confinement, it relies on external changes. The supervision and structure give offenders the opportunity to conform. And people will do what they have to do to avoid stress or enjoy pleasure. But conformity is simply not the same as lasting change or respect for law! After all, even ex-Marines commit crimes in our society!

Most individuals we put in boot camp have never experienced good role models, supervision, or discipline. Boot camp may subject them to supervision or structure for a time. But it is difficult to believe that a forty- to fifty-day period can turn around years of neglect and instill true self-discipline and self-respect.

I have visited boot camps in California, and I believe they raise ethical problems as well. We can scream in people's faces. We can move them to tears. We can frighten them with threats of extended calisthenics and the ostracism and the retaliation of their peers. But such actions don't necessarily convince people that they have any self-worth, that their life has meaning, or that they have a future. All boot camp may teach, in fact, is survival skills; offenders may get out of them and go back to what they had been doing with increased efficiency and toughness. Intensity, physical harshness, and intimidation don't change people's value systems. They may simply make them hide their real feelings deeper.

Real, lasting change comes not from external peer pressure, reward, or punishment, but from the inside out. That is why in prison ministry we believe that lasting change happens not when we beat in conformity from the outside, but when God changes a person's heart from the inside.

Would House Arrest Be More Effective?

When I toured corrections facilities in both England and Canada, I learned that those countries are using house arrest successfully. With such a high number of nonviolent offenders in America, we can give people a choice between going to prison or staying in their own community with limitations on their activities. They can continue to go to work, support their families, and pay taxes. But they lose many privileges such as going to the movies, restaurants, or bowling alleys. At the same time that offenders are under house arrest, they can work with a counselor, try to overcome drug or alcohol problems, and work on emotional problems.

In cases where the local community has doubts about the trustworthiness of a person under house arrest, electronic monitoring can be used. I have viewed such a system in Fulton, Missouri, and I believe it is a viable alternative. The monitor that is worn on the ankle is simply a radio transmitter. The computer, which keeps the police informed of the individual's whereabouts through a built-in alarm system, uses home telephone lines, and there is random calling to check on the person's location.

Some complain that the electronic bracelet is obtrusive. And at this point I would agree that it is too large, especially for women offenders, but I believe technology will soon render the device more comfortable. And when compared to the alternative—prison—the benefits of such a system clearly outweigh the drawbacks.

For example, the cost of keeping someone in a prison or a jail is much greater—eighty dollars a day compared with thirteen dollars a day on the electronic bracelet. Offenders who are still working will be able to pay restitution toward a victim or a victim's fund and even pay for the cost of the electronic monitoring. And all this is in addition to the benefit of keeping families intact, protecting nonviolent offenders from the brutalizing prison environment, reducing crowded conditions in corrections facilities, and other social and psychological benefits.

I wholeheartedly agree with the concept of house arrest. For nonviolent offenders, this form of punishment, coupled with a program of restitution and reconciliation, can be both compassionate and effective. And house arrest offers a viable way of lifting the taxpayer's burden as well by reducing the costs of incarceration.

What about Work Release?

In 1983, Cook County, Illinois, began an innovative program of alternative punishment. This program, called Sheriff's Work Alternative Program, or SWAP for short, began as a penalty program for those convicted of driving while intoxicated, then grew to cover other misdemeanors and even some felonies. It has been so successful that other counties and municipalities are considering similar programs.

SWAP combines a form of homebound detention with a work detail. Rather than going to jail, the individual lives at home but must report each day to a site where supervisors—trained sheriff's deputies—transport them to a work location. Then, wearing bright orange vests that identify them as part of the sheriff's program, and supervised by uniformed and armed sheriff's deputies, the offenders pay their debt to society through eight hours per day of labor and services. They sweep leaves and debris from sidewalks and streets. They remove graffiti from buildings. They clean streets and parks and remove rubbish, brush, and leaves from alleys.

The work-release offenders are required to show up on time, work diligently, and render good service to the community. If the work is not acceptable, they are sent home without credit for the time. And they must complete the program successfully or go to jail. They do not get paid; in fact, they must pay a fee to cover the cost of the deputies and transportation.

The most advantageous part of the program is that it costs the taxpayer absolutely nothing. In fact, the countless hours of work translates into millions of dollars in services for the community. In addition, the taxpayer saves the cost of jailing these offenders.

The offenders are penalized by the fee, the physical labor, and the embarrassment of being visibly supervised. Yet they are able to remain with their families and avoid incarceration.

Compassionate Alternatives

It is clear that warehousing people should be a scarce resource for the truly violent and for those who have committed such reprehensible crimes that they must be separated from society on a permanent basis. And these "hard cases" represent only a small percentage of the total prison population. The reality is that 94 percent of all prisoners will be released in a four-to-five-year period—and most of these will emerge from their expensive confinement the same or worse.

It is important to understand that these alternate programs of correction are not alternatives to punishment; extending compassion does not mean shortchanging justice. The programs I have described penalize offenders with limited freedom, fines or restitution, loss of property, even public embarrassment. At the same time, they offer offenders a better chance for returning to a state of responsibility and stability than traditional incarceration does, as well as saving society the cost of maintaining them in jails or prisons. For our own sake as well as the sake of the offenders, we must see that innovative, effective, and compassionate punishment is the wave of the future.

3

Christ's Call to Compassion

Alvaro Nieves

In this chapter, sociologist Alvaro Nieves emphasizes the need for compassion by pointing to the suffering that is rampant in our society—disease, injustice, violence, poverty. The theme that logically follows from his exploration of the problem is Christ's call to compassion in response to suffering. To illustrate, Dr. Nieves uses examples of Christ's own ministry and the teachings of Paul in the New Testament. He goes on to admit, however, that compassion is not a popular approach. With a poignant illustration from his own family, he shows the difficulty of reversing the effects of abuse and neglect. And he concludes with a clear choice between compassion and cynicism.

We live in a time when headlines seem to shout with suffering. All around us are people in pain. Tragedy confronts us daily, and the church is not immune.

Today, conservatively speaking, between one and one and a half million Americans are afflicted with AIDS—more than fifty thousand in the terminal stages. The death toll continues to rise. Because of the rise in AIDS among female drug users, AIDS is the ninth leading cause of death in children aged one to four. Within the next two years, at the present rate, it will be the fifth leading cause. And the social consequences of the AIDS epidemic demonstrate an absence of compassion as well. Street violence against homosexuals has increased. Infected families and children have been harassed. AIDS patients have lost their jobs. Men and women with AIDS have been denied housing and insurance. AIDS victims have become our modern-day lepers.

By 1988, nearly nine hundred thousand persons were in federal and state prisons and jails—52 percent in maximum security. At the same time, 72 percent of all of the states faced pending litigation due to overcrowding, and 14 percent have systems that have been declared unconstitutional because the overcrowding was seen as cruel and unusual punishment. Overcrowding, violence, rape, homicide, suicide—these are the characteristics of our prisons and jails. The emphasis in our penal philosophy has moved radically from rehabilitation to punishment. For every 100,000 people in the United States of America, 145 are incarcerated. Among the black population, 567 out of every 100,000 are in prison or jail.

Violence within the family is reaching epidemic proportions. Battery is the major cause of injury to women in the U.S. today. Between two thousand and four thousand women are murdered each year by husbands and lovers. Two to six million women per year are abused. A woman in the home is more likely to be injured than a police officer on the job. Elder abuse is on the increase; nearly a million senior citizens experience abuse by an adult caretaker every year. An estimated one and a half million children are abused and neglected every year. In a recent survey, 12 percent of parents reported kicking, biting, or punching their children. Three percent threatened children with a weapon, and an additional 3 percent used the weapon on a child. Murder is the fifth highest cause of death in children in the United States today. Nearly one in five girls and one in ten boys are sexually abused by the time they are eighteen years of age, and 40 percent of these are abused by a relative. Twenty-two percent of the homeless living in shelters, not including runaway shelters, are under eighteen years of age.

In 1984, a HUD study reported that an estimated sixty-six-thousand children were without adequate permanent shelter.

Recipients of Aid to Families with Dependent Children, 66 percent of whom are children, receive on the average of $3.87 per day. Recently 42 percent of the thirteen million poor children in America lived in families with incomes that were less than 50 percent of the current poverty line.

In a day when there is evidence of so much pain and so much suffering, Christ calls his people and his church to compassion. He does this in at least three ways—through the Word, as our model, and as our teacher.

Compassion in Scripture

Scripture calls us to compassion by revealing something of the mind or the attitude of Christ. And Paul admonishes us in a well-known passage in Philippians:

> "Your attitude should be the same as that of Christ Jesus: Who, being in very nature God, did not consider equality with God something to be grasped, but made himself nothing, taking the very nature of a servant, being made in human likeness. And being found in appearance as a man, he humbled himself and became obedient to death—even death on a cross." (Phil. 2:5–8)

This passage, to me, sets forth the essence of biblical compassion: the call to compassion is a call to suffer. The Latin roots of the word compassion consist of two words: *cum,* meaning "with" and *pati,* meaning "suffer." Compassion, in other words, literally means "to suffer with." In a little book called *Compassion,* the authors write:

> Compassion asks us to go where it hurts, to enter into places of pain, to share in brokenness and fear, confusion and anguish. Compassion challenges us to cry out with those in misery, to mourn with those who are lonely, to weep with those in tears. Compassion requires us to be weak with the weak, vulnerable with the vulnerable and powerless with the powerless. Compassion means full immersion in the conditions of being human.

Compassion as used in the Scripture is usually translated in a number of different ways—sometimes as "mercy," sometimes as "pity," sometimes as "tenderness." In the New Testament, the Greek verb literally means a movement of the entrails or the bowels, which were considered the seat of the emotions. We use the same idea today when we talk about a "gut-wrenching experience." The Hebrew word for compassion in the Old Testament carries similar connotations. In fact, it is often used to refer to the womb, sometimes to the womb of God. It conveys a deep cherishing, tender love, mercy, pity. When God is moved with compassion, in other words, he is moved to the very center and essence of his being.

When the Bible speaks of compassion, it is clearly not talking about a passing or whimsical concern, a sympathy we can communicate through the use of a greeting card. Compassion is gut-wrenching. It changes lives.

Look again at the tough-minded compassion to which the Scriptures call us to: Administer true justice. Show mercy and compassion to one another. Do not oppress the widow or the fatherless, the alien, or the poor. Do not think evil of each other in your hearts. Jesus says, "Be compassionate as your Father is compassionate" (Luke 6:36). And the apostle Paul, writing of the "new creature" we become in Christ, exhorts us, "As God's chosen people, holy and dearly loved, clothe yourselves with compassion, kindness, humility, gentleness, and patience" (Col. 3:12).

Jesus—Model of Compassion

Compassion is clearly among the traits Christ exemplified for us during his life here on earth as a human being. Let's look at a few instances from his earthly ministry to get a clear picture of the kind of compassion he was modeling for us.

Mark 6:34 tells us of a time when Jesus and his disciples had tried to get away for a rest, only to be followed by a great crowd. What was his attitude? "When Jesus landed and saw a large crowd, he had compassion on them, because they were like sheep without a shepherd. So he began teaching them many things." What was Jesus' attitude toward the crowd? Compassion. And what was his response? He took the opportunity to teach.

In Matthew 14, we again see Jesus withdrawing to a solitary place but being followed by a crowd. What happened? "He had

compassion on them." This time, however, he responded by healing their sick.

In Matthew 15:32 and Mark 8:2, Jesus called to his disciples after ministering for three days to four thousand people who had
come to him for healing and teaching. He said, in essence, "I feel
compassion for these people because they are hungry." And what
did he do? He fed them.

In encounter after encounter—with a leper (Mark 1:41), with
two blind men (Matt. 20:34), with a woman whose son had died
(Luke 7:13), with a demon-possessed man (Mark 5:19)—we see
the pattern of Jesus' compassion and his helping response. In each
case, Jesus was moved to compassion by varying degrees of human pain. And in each case, his response was both direct and appropriate to the circumstance. He responded to people's pain and
then met them where they were. In so doing, he gave us a useful
model for responding to the suffering we perceive around us.

Jesus—Teacher of Compassion

Christ calls us to compassion not only through his Word and
his example, but through his teaching. In the parable of the un-
merciful servant, for instance, Jesus teaches about the importance of compassionate forgiveness.

You know the story, told in Matthew 18. It compares the kingdom of heaven to a king who wants to settle accounts with his
servants. One servant owes him ten thousand talents, the equivalent of about ten million dollars, and cannot pay. So the master
orders that the servant, his wife, his children, and all that he has
be sold to repay the debt. The servant falls on his knees before his
master. "Be patient with me," he begs, "and I will pay back everything." And the master takes pity on him—that word for "pity" is
translated elsewhere as compassion. He cancels the debt and lets
the servant go.

You remember what happens next. The servant who was forgiven his debt encounters a fellow servant, who owes him something on the order of twenty dollars and has him thrown into
debtor's prison. Word gets back to the master, who is furious. He
has the first servant thrown in jail and tortured until he pays his
debt.

We usually think of this parable as a commentary on forgiveness, but there's more to it than that. The source of forgiveness in the story is compassion.

The second parable that concerns forgiveness is also a very familiar one—the Good Samaritan. Here is what one Baptist preacher had to say about that story:

> One day a man came to Jesus and he said to him, "Who is my neighbor?" That question could have easily ended in a philosophical and theological debate. But Jesus immediately pulled that question from midair and placed it on a dangerous curve, between Jerusalem and Jericho. The Jericho Road is a dangerous road. The first question that the priest asked, the first question that the Levite asked was, If I stop to help this man what will happen to me? But then the Good Samaritan came by and reversed the question. "If I do *not* stop to help this man, what will happen to him?"

That Baptist preacher was Dr. Martin Luther King, Jr. It was part of a sermon he presented in Memphis, Tennessee, just two nights before he was assassinated. And it speaks to us just as vitally today as it did to those present in 1968.

The key verse for us is Luke 10:33. "But a certain Samaritan, who was on a journey, came upon him"—the injured man. "And when he saw him, he felt compassion" (NASB).

You see, that was a different response. The robbers beat the man up. The priest and the Levite passed him by. But the Good Samaritan had compassion and helped him.

The response of the church to people today is not usually a struggle between all three choices, because we reject the first. Too often, however, we get stuck on the second. We need to make a choice between passing up and picking up. And it's not always an easy choice.

Compassion—A Tough Mandate

The call to compassion, my friends, my brother and sisters, is not a popular one—especially in our society where we are moved by the desire to avoid pain at almost any cost. Where we are driven by a narcissistic urge to fulfill our least desires. Where we live by mottos, "You deserve a break today," and "Have it your way."

All too often, we are tempted to ignore the commandments of God to be a compassionate church and a compassionate people. And yet, as we have seen, Christ is still calling us to compassion. Compassion is as much our mandate as the mandate to do justice. Indeed, sometimes the two are combined. We cannot do justice without compassion.

Marion Wright Ettleman, writing as an advocate for children in her book, *The Family in Peril,* eloquently calls us to active, responsive compassion:

> I worry about men and women who refuse to take a position because of the complexity or controversy that often surrounds issues of life and death. I hold no brief for those who are content to kibitz intellectually about the life choices of millions of poor children without seeing the hunger and the suffering behind the cold statistics, or for those who hide behind professional neutrality and shift responsibility for hard social problems to others, problems that must be shared if they are to be solved. Feeding a hungry child or preventing needless infant deaths in a decent rich society should not require detailed policy analysis or quantifiable outcome goals or endless commissions or committees. They require compassionate action.

I want to tell you about my own family so you will understand how the study of compassion has been difficult for me.

God has blessed us with six children. Five of those children are adopted, and none of them were adopted as infants. All came from troubled, abusive backgrounds. My oldest daughter was taken from her birth parent for the last time when she was hospitalized because her mother hit her on the head with a hammer. And that was simply the culmination of years of physical and sexual and psychological abuse.

Today, as a consequence of that earlier suffering, I have two children who are in treatment. One, at age seventeen a ward of the juvenile court, has been away from our family now for over a year. Changing that young life is going to take a miracle. My youngest son, a half brother of his older brother biologically, full brother by adoption, is struggling now in hospital care to overcome the consequences of his earlier abuse.

We see in our children the visitation of sins of the fathers. And I will tell you what all of you already know, that the pain of having a child whom you somehow can't reach can do one of two things. It can either harden you to an impermeable cynicism, or it can make you compassionate.

Once we have been struck by personal suffering at this level, it becomes extremely difficult to be judgmental—to be anything but compassionate to our brothers and our sisters in need.

Let me conclude with a short poem by Nancy Telfer:

I listen to the agony of God, I who am fed,
Who never yet went hungry for a day.
I see the dead, the children starved for lack of bread,
I see, and try to pray.
I listen to the agony of God, I who am warm,
Who never yet lacked for a sheltering home.
In dull alarm, the dispossessed of hut and farm,
Aimless and transient roam.
I listen to the agony of God,
I who am strong with health and love and laughter in my soul.
I see a throng of stunted children, reared in wrong,
And wish to make them whole.
I listen to the agony of God,
But know full well not until I share their bitter cry,
Earth's pain and hell, can God within my spirit dwell.
To bring the kingdom nigh.

4

The Ministry of Justice

Daniel Van Ness

As an attorney, Dan Van Ness did significant legal work for the poor. This experience gave him a special sensitivity for indigent people entrapped in the criminal justice system. For many years now, however, he has been president of Justice Fellowship, an organization that seeks to permeate the system with Christian principles.

Mr. Van Ness begins his chapter with the harsh reality that the prison population has grown fifteen times faster than the population of our country. He believes this population explosion is closely tied to harsh mandatory sentencing laws that in turn reflect the public's rising anger about crime. But on a deeper level, he claims, the changes reflect the fact that we've lost the "soul of justice"—the sense and reason that lie behind the law. As a result, the public's anger and vengeance have been unleashed, and the criminal justice system has become myopically focused on technique rather than substance.

To correct this situation, Van Ness believes, we need to reexamine our concepts of what justice is. And the church has the opportunity to contribute significantly to this redefinition. For we serve a God whose justice is based in love, whose purpose in dealing justice is to reestablish harmony in the community and health in the individual. Our call as Christians is to involve ourselves in establishing that kind of love-based justice in our criminal justice system today.

The United States Census Bureau just released its report of the growth in the number of inmates in prisons, jails, and detention facilities over the last ten years. In 1980 there were 450,000 men and women in prison. In 1990 there were 1,150,000. This means that the prison population has more than doubled in the last decade. The prison population grew fifteen times faster than the general population during that time.

We are just now becoming aware of the tremendous toll this growth is exacting on our society. For the last seven years, prisons have been the fastest growing item in state budgets across the country. The cost of corrections is growing twice as fast as that of primary education, twice as fast as secondary education, four times as fast as medical care for the elderly and poor. It now costs an average of $17,000 a year to house a single inmate. These are direct costs and do not include such indirect costs as lost taxes and welfare support.

Why have we seen this explosion in prison population? In large part, it results not from better apprehension of criminals but of legislation that takes discretion away from judges and that mandates longer, more severe sentences. This is especially true for drug offenses. In fact, the population explosion in federal prisons can be directly traced to changes in drug offense sentencing laws. (This is happening in state prisons as well.)

These reforms stem from rising public anger over crime, and they are supported by the public. A recent poll found that 55 percent of the public feel sentences are too lenient, 37 percent feel they are adequate, and only 8 percent feel they are too harsh.

There is some debate, however, over whether crime itself has actually risen in the last decade. Some victimization studies show that it stayed basically stable. But the FBI compilation of *reported* crimes has gone up every year. So we can say at least that *reported* crime has increased—that the public is more willing to report crime. They are willing to support tough sentences to crack down on criminals. We see that at every election year. And they even appear willing to accept *some* increase in taxes to support that. One poll claimed that 62 percent of the public indicated that they would agree to higher taxes if doing so would solve the crime problem.

This move to incarcerate more people, to lock them up in warehouses, is logical if we have lost hope that people can change. But if we have, our loss of hope leads to horrible implications for society. Why? The criminal justice system is collapsing under its own weight and threatens to bring down government with it.

In Los Angeles County, people literally get lost in the jail. A pastor I know went to visit a parishioner. The superintendent of the jail said, "Yes, we know he must be here, but we can't find him in our computer. Come back in two days; we will have found him by then."

Across the country, states are letting prisoners out the back door in order to let new offenders in the front door. Once out, scarce dollars means they receive little supervision. In Illinois, 176 probation officials were just furloughed, 140 of them in Chicago. What that means is that supervision being provided to offenders when they come out of prison has been dramatically curtailed.

We're losing the ability, or maybe the desire, to distinguish between offenders who pose a danger to the community and those who do not. Forty-seven percent of the people in state prisons across the country are there for nonviolent crimes. Thirty-five percent have *never* committed a violent crime. And yet we're releasing violent offenders early in order to make room for this kind of population.

Have We Lost the "Soul of Justice"?

For ten years, Justice Fellowship, the reform arm of Prison Fellowship, has worked with Christian citizens and other public officials to address these problems. We've promoted alternatives to incarceration for nonviolent offenders as a way of preserving prison space for the people who need to be there, restoring the victim through restitution, and restoring the offender through meaningful accountability. These alternatives give offenders the opportunity to pay their debt.

We have found that there are effective strategies for changing laws, even when public sentiment seems to favor the opposite of what we call for.

We have also discovered that public officials believe the problem is much more fundamental than a few laws can correct. The attorney general in a major state told us that his criminal justice system is beyond salvaging and in need of total overhaul.

When Daniel Boone was old and about to die, he was asked whether he had ever gotten lost on one of his expeditions. Old Daniel thought about it for a while and said, "No, I can't ever recall having been lost. But I do remember once being *perplexed* for three days."

Like Daniel Boone, I think there is a difference between being lost and being perplexed. Being perplexed means that while you are not sure where you are, *you know what to do* to get yourself out of that predicament. Being lost means that you are so overwhelmed by your predicament that *you must simply wait* for someone to come and get you.

In the area of criminal justice, this country is fast moving beyond being perplexed to becoming lost. We have lost our sense of direction. Or to put it another way, we have lost the soul of justice.

A sixteenth-century judge wrote, "Law is divided into two parts: a body and a soul. The body of the law is the letter of the law, and the soul of the law is its sense and reason."

When we lose our sense and reason, or our sense of direction, we often fall back on technique. When I was growing up, I was told, "If you are ever lost in the woods, don't delude yourself into thinking you can walk straight. What happens is you walk in circles and eventually get worn out."

But the instinct to do something is hard to resist. And in criminal justice, "do something" translates into longer sentences, tougher sentences, mandatory sentences. Ironically, predictably, that just makes the situation worse.

Erosion of Concern

The soul of justice in the United States used to be *concern for the offender.* Rehabilitation gave purpose to the criminal justice system and led to the development of our familiar institutions of criminal justice: the penitentiary (literally a "place of penitence"), the parole system, the probation system, juvenile courts, and so on. All these institutions were created out of concern to rehabilitate the offender.

Many polls still demonstrate tremendous below-the-surface public support for rehabilitation. I have even talked to victims who have said, "If I could be certain that something done for this person would mean that he would not do it again, I would be interested in seeing him sentenced to that sort of program."

Rehabilitation offered hope, and it helped curb our natural inclination to be vengeful and vindictive against those who violate us and our laws. But over the last twenty years, policy makers and practitioners have largely abandoned the rehabilitation theory.

There are a variety of reasons for this change. One is that rehabilitation didn't appear to work; a number of programs turned out to have minimal impact on recidivism. Second, it failed to protect the community. Neighborhoods, concerned about rising crime rates, could not understand spending money to give offenders an education (for example) while crime rates soared. Third, rehabilitation failed to respond to the needs of victims who very justly accused the criminal justice system of being more interested in offenders than in victims, and of providing services to offenders that are never offered to victims.

I think there have been two results for us as a society. One is that our anger at and fear of criminals has been unleashed. No longer restrained by any effort to make them better, we now are satisfied simply to punish them harder. Second, because we have found no alternate way to demonstrate concern for offenders, what concern we have gets focused on technique.

The prevailing sentencing theory today is something called "the just deserts" theory. It's the principle of proportionality: everybody should be sentenced comparably with other offenders and consistently with the crime he or she has committed.

There is nothing wrong with fairness. As Christians, we favor it. But fairness by itself cannot be the soul of justice.

A friend of mine asked me one day, "What happens when you combine a Jehovah's Witness with an atheist?" Well, I didn't know. It turns out that when you combine a Jehovah's Witness with an atheist, you get someone who knocks on your door for no reason.

Learning to knock rhythmically is no substitute for knowing what to say when the door opens. Learning to be exactly fair in sentencing is no substitute for not knowing the purpose of sentencing, any more than punishing children exactly the same can substitute for knowing the purpose of child raising.

Redefining Justice

Do we have anything to offer? Can the church perform a ministry of justice in a criminal justice system rapidly losing its soul?

I think we can. After all, justice is a dimension of God's character. Justice is a *Person* before it is a concept—and he expects it to be a part of the character of his people as well.

As we look at Scripture, we learn things about the question of justice: what it means, what it is intended to do. We discover that justice is related to *shalom.* Crime violates *shalom,* and the biblical purpose of punishment is to repair that violation through restitution.

What is *shalom?* It is wholeness and completeness in the community. It is reconciled relationships, harmony, and concord. *Shalom* is the state of right relationship between God and humanity and within communities. Isn't it interesting that when confronted by the very thing that is tearing our communities apart—crime—the biblical response is to build communities characterized by *shalom?*

How is it possible that justice could bring *shalom,* harmonious relationships? Isn't justice dispassionate and objective, aloof? Isn't our image of justice a cool goddess, blindfolded to maintain neutrality?

Isaiah 59 presents a very different image:

> The Lord looked and was displeased
>   that there was no justice.
> He saw that there was no one,
>   he was appalled that there was no one to intervene;
> so his own arm worked salvation for him,
>   and his own righteousness sustained him.
> He put on righteousness as his breastplate,
>   and the helmet of salvation on his head;
> he put on the garment of vengeance

and wrapped himself in zeal as in a cloak.
According to what they have done,
  so will he repay
wrath to his enemies
  and retribution to his foes;
  he will repay the islands their due.
From the west, men will fear the name of the Lord,
  and from the rising of the sun, they will revere his glory.
For he will come like a pent-up flood
  that the breath of the Lord drives along.
"The Redeemer will come to Zion,
  to those in Jacob who repent of their sins,"
    declares the Lord.

(Isa. 59:15–20)

Note the passionate words that describe God's response to injustice. He was *displeased,* he was *appalled* that there was no one to intervene. He put on garments of *vengeance* and wrapped himself in *zeal.* He repaid *wrath* and *retribution.* He comes like a *pent-up flood* in order to establish justice.

Justice in the Bible is passionate. And why is God so passionate? What motivates him to become personally involved? Listen to these hopeful words from Jeremiah:

I have loved you with an everlasting love;
  I have drawn you with loving-kindness.
I will build you up again and you will be rebuilt.

(Jer. 31:3)

This leads me to wonder if the soul of justice, the thing that gives it life, is love. I almost hesitate to say this because I know the predictable response. "Give me a break!" many would say. "Crime and injustice bring devastation, and all you have to offer is sentimentality. You just don't understand the problem."

The difficulty is not that we don't understand the problem, but that we don't understand love. The powerful love of God leads to actions that sometimes appear paradoxical. On some occasions, his love leads him to put on armor and wade into battle and wreak vengeance on his enemy. On other occasions it leads him to take off his armor, walk into battle, stretch out his arms, and be crucified.

Earlier I used the example of parenting to ridicule the idea that fairness or equality is the sole purpose of justice. Parents understand that sometimes love is tough and sometimes love is tender, but love always preserves the personhood of the beloved and seeks his or her ultimate good. Can we say that about our criminal justice system?

Handcuffs of Love

I had an opportunity several weeks ago to visit a prison in Brazil run by volunteers affiliated with Prison Fellowship Brazil. It is an extraordinary prison—different from anything any of us have experienced. Inmates open the doors; they have the keys. Security as we understand it is totally compromised. When an inmate needs to leave the premises to go to court, that inmate is escorted by other inmates.

The staff is made up entirely of volunteers. It is overseen by the judge responsible for all of the prisons in that area, and the judge is supported because this prison is incredibly productive and stable. It is the cleanest prison I have ever seen. The cleaning schedule is established and carried out by the inmates.

We asked inmates why they stayed when they could just walk away. Some had been assigned to other prisons and had tried for years to get assigned to this one because they believed they could escape easily. But one inmate expressed the reason for his presence eloquently: "When I walked into this prison, they took off handcuffs of steel and replaced them with handcuffs of love."

The philosophy of this prison is, "Kill the criminal and save the man," and the method for doing that is love. One of the founders of the prison explained to me the philosophy of this prison, the principles behind it: "Crime is the violent and tragic refusal to love. We were created to love. God made us so that he could love us and so we could love him and each other. Why is it, if we were made for love and to love, that we find love so difficult?"

He went on to suggest that love is like other abilities—to speak, to write, to play the violin—in that it is a *latent* ability. We have the capacity, but we can't use it until someone teaches us how. The apprenticeship for love is meant to be served in the family. But too often, because of sin and corruption, the family is incapable of teaching us how to love. So what the volunteers in this Brazilian prison have done is to create a family.

What difference would it make in our own country if we looked at crime with eyes of love as we arm ourselves to do justice?

First we would have to show that there are different ways of responding. We would have to restore hope in this society that people can indeed change, because when hope is gone, all that is left is the impulse for revenge. Victims and offenders are not faceless, nameless individuals who make us uncomfortable. They are *people*. Seeing their faces and calling their names is part of our job in doing justice.

Second, we need to change the system. We need to start viewing crime as *injury* and not simply as lawbreaking. It involves injury to victims, to the community, even to offenders—and injury requires healing as well as justice. We also need to respond differently to both victims and offenders. We need to hold offenders accountable and to find appropriate ways for victims to participate in the process.

The difference between being lost and being perplexed is that when you are lost you have to wait for someone to come get you. When it comes to criminal justice in America, our nation is fast becoming hopelessly lost. God is calling us to respond; to give direction. Let us do so at once.

Part 3

Our Biblical Mandate
to Minister to Hurting People

Introduction

We live in an increasingly disposable society. Built-in obsolescence is a reality of Western manufacturing. At fast-food restaurants, everything from the plastic utensils and straws to the hamburger carton has a life of approximately fifteen minutes.

The cultural rule is quite simple: When a product outlives its usefulness, throw it away!

Imagine seeing a paper cup lying in a gutter. It has treadmarks on it and is mostly crushed. You would not attempt to repair it because it is not meant to be repaired. And even if the cup were not crushed, would you want to drink out of it? The obvious answer is no.

When we label something as refuse or garbage, the only thing left to do is to dispose of it, take it out of sight, and never see or use it again.

In 1985, the Institute for Prison Ministries hosted an inmate art contest. Of the more than forty pieces it acquired, one was most intriguing. Many people thought it overly simplistic and could not figure it out. The painting, mostly done in tones of grey, was of a stack of discarded styrofoam cups. Those cups take on their deeper, symbolic significance only when we realize that it was a prisoner who painted it.

Clearly, prisoners in our society are treated as the human equivalent of garbage. They are rejected. They are removed from sight. Many have completely lost their sense of purpose and usefulness.

The Billy Graham Center on the Wheaton College campus is a magnificent and stately building. The lawns and shrubbery are manicured. The surrounding suburb has good schools and a multitude of large churches. And yet who would guess that within a fifty-mile radius of a city that was once voted "the all-American town," there are almost sixteen hundred prisoners? Obviously we do not see what we do not want to see.

An Inescapable Call

I remember having a conversation with a pastor who said to me, "I don't feel our church is called to prison ministry."

I was personally astounded by that comment. I inquired, "What Bible are you reading?" I did not mean to sound condescending. What I meant was that the Bible could not be clearer about the mission that Jesus gave the church in ministering to hurting people in general, and prisoners in particular. In the account of the last judgment found in Matthew 25, prisoners are named specifically. In Hebrews 13, too, Paul tells us to have compassion and empathy with prisoners.

The biblical mandate to visit prisoners is inescapable. The problem is that people are often waiting for the right emotional climate; they equate emotions with a sense of calling. But it does not matter whether you are excited or apprehensive about ministering to prisoners, whether you have a mixture of emotions, or you simply don't know what you feel. Emotions come and go, and they may or may not match our need to feel comfortable or happy. The key issue is obedience to the Word of God. As servants we are judged on our faithfulness.

Every member of the church is called to prison ministry, but not necessarily in the same way. Clearly people are called according to their gifts. Some may feel comfortable visiting inmates. Others may encourage prisoners through letters. I know volunteers who meet inmates only when they grade their Bible correspondence-course papers. Everyone, however, should play a role in trying to help released Christian ex-offenders make the transition back into the community by helping them find a church and feel welcome.

I was recently at a meeting where neighbors were upset about a halfway house on their block. It would be used for Christian ex-offenders. I perfectly understood their reasonable fears, but I was very disappointed by the level of irrational behavior. Adults actually yelled and screamed, "We don't want you! Go away!" Individuals used examples of worst-case scenarios, implying that child molesters and serial murderers would be living on their block. And I know that some of these protesters were Christians.

The sad fact is that there really is no community in America you could approach with a proposition of a transitional living facility for ex-offenders and receive any form of positive reception. Intelligent people applaud the concept of helping released inmates toward stability, but no one is willing to take a risk.

This is why the biblical mandate to minister to hurting people is specifically for the church. I believe the church, more than any other segment of society, especially government, is uniquely equipped to help those the world treats as garbage. And this applies specifically to offenders within our institutions and ex-offenders upon release.

Take Down the Barriers

Clearly, the church also has a mandate for world evangelism, and foreign missions is an established part of every church's budget. But I believe most churches have failed to balance foreign missions and domestic concerns.

A friend recently told me, with obvious pleasure on his face, that he had been trying to get his church to raise twenty thousand dollars to build a well in an African country. "We were able to raise forty-two thousand!" he exclaimed, then went on to say, "Now we can build two wells." I am sure that the African well was truly needed. But this church's local community also needed a halfway house for ex-offenders, a program for battered wives, and drug education and rehabilitation programs. I am quite confident that no one suggested taking the additional twenty-two thousand dollars and putting it to use in the local community.

I believe there is one explanation for the imbalance between local ministry and foreign missions, and I do not mean to be cynical: sometimes foreign missions is safer. Giving money to a faraway project need not involve direct service or relationships. The chances of someone from ten thousand miles away showing up on your doorstep tomorrow morning is remote. But when we become involved on our own block, in our own community, we can easily be inconvenienced.

People who are hurting have needs—medical care, food, clothes, transportation. At times, I believe, American churches have looked upon the poor as a burden. I have heard church people say that the welfare system is responsible for the poor. But this is not what the Bible says. I have heard people say, "We'd be happy to have an ex-offender in our church," but make no attempt to identify and invite someone.

Over 80 percent of all Christian ex-offenders never find a home church. This is partly due to a cultural and intellectual barrier similar to the architectural barriers Joni Eareckson Tada has told me about. For someone who is wheelchair bound, the very sight of a church with steps and no ramp becomes a sign that the disabled person is not welcome.

Pastors have told Joni, "If disabled people came to our church, then we would build a ramp." Her response is, "If you really want them in your church, build the ramp first. Then they will come."

There are churches where middle-class people dress very well and where the messages tend to be weighted on the side of intellectualism. Many ex-offenders and their families do not have good clothes. Many people are functionally illiterate. But instead of adapting our churches to include them, we have created cultural barriers that make them feel as unwelcome as architectural barriers do to a person in a wheelchair.

How do we adapt? The starting point is to realize that our biblical mandate to help hurting people is not an elective. Once we understand that this is the very heart of the church's mission and work, then we can begin to make natural adaptations. And we can begin opening our eyes—and our arms—to those who are suffering.

Responsible for One Another

Several years ago I spoke in San Quentin Prison. As I was about to leave, a young inmate named Andrew approached me. He said, "I've been following Jesus for three months." I was polite, but the conversation lacked energy. I hadn't treated his statement with much enthusiasm. Normally, when someone says he or she has been a Christian for thirty years, we light up, but three months is hardly anything to celebrate.

The chaplain approached me and said, "I saw you talking to Andrew." "Yes," I replied. "Do you know much about him?" the chaplain inquired. "Not really," I answered. The chaplain then informed me, "For the past two years, Andrew was a drag queen in the prison. He wore women's makeup, and his body was used, bartered, and traded among the inmates." Now, having affirmed himself as a disciple of Jesus, he had to depend daily on the physical protection of his Christian brothers. He was not able to walk across the prison yard without former abusers' calling and whistling and making threatening or derogatory comments.

Perhaps Andrew's faith initially is no more than a smoldering wick, yet God promises he will not snuff it out (Isa. 42:3; Matt. 12:20). In prison, surely his life is in danger as he tries to radically change from a sinful to a holy life. If Andrew were to get out of prison, imagine how much care and nurturing he would need from the church.

In another prison, when a chaplain made an invitation to accept Christ at a service I attended, I saw a young Hispanic prisoner named James come forward. Unlike the great crusades of Billy Graham, this altar call yielded only the single prisoner. I was sitting close to him. I noticed that he was so nervous he was trembling. It occurred to me that the Holy Spirit had prompted him to make the decision, but he didn't know the implications of following Jesus. What he did know was that starting the next day he would still be tempted by drugs, in danger from the gangs and the violence, and he didn't know if he had the strength to endure.

It was at that point the chaplain said to the other eighty prisoners in the chapel, "Do you remember when your mother came home from the hospital with a new baby brother and said you must be careful and gentle because he is very fragile, that as he grows up you must hold his hand and guide him and teach him and protect him?" He then turned James until facing his brothers in Christ in this prison and said, "This is your new baby brother, James! You must protect him in the yard! You must teach him the Bible! He is fragile, so you must be kind and gentle and even willing to lay down your life to protect him!"

I've never heard such a profound illustration of community and the body of Christ. We are responsible for each other, beyond a superficial sense. The chaplain said it correctly; we bear an intimate responsibility to each other as disciples.

In prison, people like Andrew need Christian brothers who will nurture and protect them. When they are released from prison, they will need a church that will do the same. Without such a support system, a new Christian can easily fall by the wayside. We have a mandate from God's Word to reach out to hurting people, specifically to prisoners.

5

Religious Diversity and the Christian Response

Charles Riggs

Charles Riggs, the chief of chaplains for the United States federal system, has encountered wide religious diversity in his work of ministering to inmates. He begins his chapter by describing some of the religious and cultural groups that fill our societies—and our prisons—and tracing some of the church's past involvement in prisons. He goes on to acknowledge that Christians who minister in prisons often face the dilemma of presenting the claims of Christ to people of diverse religious backgrounds while at the same time respecting their culture and their freedom to choose.

With this background, Chaplain Riggs attempts to describe a strategy whereby Christians can minister effectively and with integrity in a climate of religious diversity. He calls the church to compassion and involvement, stating clearly that we can allow for diversity without compromising the distinctive message of Jesus Christ. He proclaims that those in ministry should not be apologetic about their faith but meet people where they are, trusting God to do the rest. He concludes that religious diversity in our prisons is a fact we should not fear.

The religious diversity that used to be described in comparative religion textbooks is now a reality in our hometowns. People of many different faiths live and work side by side in many of our communities—and our prisons and jails are no exceptions. In the institutions where I minister, some of us have learned to pronounce names and deal with customs we never knew existed.

We have Rastafarians, with their dreadlocks and reggae music and Jamaican accents, who worship Haile Selasse as the Lion of Judah—their messiah.

And we have Sikhs, with their turban-wrapped heads and tiny silver swords and neatly kept beards. Their "white baptism" declares that they will always be willing to give their lives in defense of their holy sites.

We also have members of the Original Black Hebrew Israelites of Jerusalem, who see themselves as the lost tribe of Israel. This group has maintained property in Israel and established themselves as the completion of all historical prophecy, claiming to be both fully Jewish and fully Christian. Although they accept Jesus Christ as a messiah, theirs is an eclectic faith that attempts to bring all truth into one belief system. They are a very difficult group to manage in prison—not because they are violent, but because of some of their practices. They are the only group I know of that keep a kosher vegetarian diet, which means they almost have to be in the free world to get the nutrients they need.

Santeria, a faith that has crept up from the Caribbean, is well represented in certain prisons. It combines Roman Catholicism with a touch of nature worship, sometimes voodooism, sometimes the occult. Followers of Santeria adopt special forms of dress and may be heavily involved with animalistic forces, the worship of nature, and the powers of darkness.

There has been a resurgence of Hasidic Judaism, the ultra-orthodox fundamentalist form of the faith, in many of our cities. Since in any large community you will find some who break the law, we also have a Hasidic population in our prisons. Hasidic Jews are extremely difficult to provide for in prison because of their intricate system of religious rules. In one instance in our own system, we rented the entire penal institution to a Hasidic

Jew for twenty-five cents a year. This means he could count the entire institution as his home. And this was important because he was not allowed to carry any object outside his home on the Sabbath. In this institution the cells were separate from the restrooms and the inmates were issued their own rolls of toilet paper. He could not carry his roll to the restroom unless the entire institution was considered his home.

The religion of Islam is well represented in our prisons, just as it is in our communities. The number of Muslims has grown to five million adherents in this nation, and some of these have been incarcerated.

And linked with Islam is the Nation of Islam, a black militant reaction to American culture and society that began in the thirties with Elijah Mohammad and is now carried on by Louis Farrakhan. This particular variety of Islam has a very nationalistic orientation and borders at times on being a hate group of black against white. In contrast—and sometimes in violent confrontation—is the Aryan Church of Jesus Christ Christian, a white supremacist organization. This group, which claims to be Christian, is more and more prevalent in our prisons.

This introduction is just to give you a sense of the religious diversity that characterizes our society—and as a reflection of society, our prisons. Many of these religions have come to America speaking different languages, wearing different clothes, and espousing different values than those of mainstream America. This diversity of religion is closely linked with a new diversity of culture. And increasingly we are called—by Christian brothers and sisters as well as by others—to overcome narrow cultural boundaries, respect religious differences, and learn to coexist in a pluralistic society.

What does this mean to prison ministry? Since most prison ministry in this country is related to the Christian community, it means a challenge to reach into the creative bag to find ways to get across cultural and religious barriers in order to share the gospel with the men and women who people our corrections organizations. It also means formulating an acceptable response to those who accuse us of trying to force an alien religion and an alien culture on those from different backgrounds.

The Church Stands By

The preponderance of prison ministry in this country is related to the Christian community. And that's to be expected. Throughout the history of corrections, the church has always been standing close by. The church has always been standing by in the history of corrections—from the first day when Pope Clement XI established the cell-type reformatory where young people could be sent to ponder the error of their ways and be provided for while they did penance. That first penitentiary in 1711 was an outgrowth of the church's concern.

Eleven years later, across the Atlantic, the church stood by at the Walnut Street Jail in Philadelphia, where Quakers took a stand against the standard punishments of the day. "Enough of this public punishment of sinners," they said. "Enough of this hanging. Enough of this putting prisoners in stocks in the center of the square. Enough of this dunking. Punishment ought to be private." To translate those protests into action, they established the first penitentiary on American soil. And the church stood by.

After awhile, the people from the church did say, "But you can't leave prisoners there in solitary confinement to do penance. They're bored. Their minds and spirits and social skills will atrophy. You must give them work to do." So the church stood by while they opened up rock quarries and road gangs.

After a bit we had a conscience pang and said, "Well, this surely isn't the whole story. Putting inmates to work isn't really helping all that much, because people who commit crimes are really sick. We must cure them. And when they are well, they can go home." And the church stood by, nodded, and said, "Maybe that's it."

Then we reached the point where we said, "The cure rate is very low. Sixty-seven percent recidivism means prisons aren't curing the prisoners; they haven't solved the problem." And the church stood by, uninvolved.

Criminologists suggested, "What we need to do now is to incapacitate prisoners, to warehouse them, to set prisoners aside so they will not create any more problems in the community." So the prisons swelled, and the church stood by.

Then we said, "Well, maybe what we need to do is to find a way somehow to rehabilitate prisoners. If we do, we will be able to put them back in society. Then they can join the rest of us in straightening out our world." The church still was not prodded to action.

We now begin to talk about an emerging theme of reintegration into society with a clarification of values. Prisoners can choose, from a diversity of approaches, those which will help them in their approach to life. And the church is still standing by, waiting, doing little to help the situation in current times.

Responding to Diversity

But you in prison ministry, who have come out of the church and are motivated by the church, sometimes have difficulty understanding why all the church isn't fully with you—why your fellow Christians accuse you of not respecting the diversity of cultures and religions you encounter. How can you respond to the questions that cultural pluralism and religious diversity raise? How can you remain true to the Great Commission while respecting those of other cultures and other religions?

As a Christian and as a minister, I am called to the task of bringing the gospel to those who have not heard it, including those of other religions. I am also entrusted with the spiritual well-being of a number of inmates from a diversity of religious and cultural backgrounds, and it is my job to nurture and help them regardless of how they worship. Out of this experience, I have become convinced that there is a way to respond with fairness, faith, and integrity to these diversity issues.

Without Apology

First, responding to diversity need not mean compromising our values, our beliefs, or our mission. Addressing diversity doesn't mean that we put off that which is our identity. Without apology or justification, we can hold to these distinctives of Christian belief and ministry:

That the only genuine rehabilitation of the heart comes through acceptance of Jesus Christ as personal Lord and Savior. "Create in me a clean heart, O God." (Ps. 51:10 NASB)

> That the only genuine reorganization of a personality is a new design by Christ: "If any man is in Christ, he is a new creature." (2 Cor. 5:17 NASB)
>
> That the only lasting motivation to change an antisocial lifestyle is derived from imitating Christ in character and conduct. "The old order of things has passed away." (Rev. 21:4)
>
> That the only source for healing the mind and spirit is the indwelling presence of Christ. "Let this mind be in you which was also in Christ Jesus." (Phil. 2:5 NKJV)

As Christians in prison ministry who want to be sensitive to diversity issues, we don't have to offer any apology for believing these things, or for sharing the joyous victory in the lives of people. All we have to do is to share these things with a spirit of openness and honesty—to be ourselves in Christ.

A little group of prisoners that I knew well in the penitentiary in Atlanta came to me one day and said, "Preacher, you've got to do something about Lucky. We're afraid for him."

Lucky happened to be in the really tough cellhouse, and until recently he had been an especially tough case himself—doing life plus twenty-five for the murder of a United States marshal. He had already been in for a very long time, and he had had no relationship of any kind with anyone on the staff. Then we had gotten the news that Lucky's mother had died. The chaplain broke the news to him and offered to help. He didn't even acknowledge that simple offer of help, but it got something started.

We had held a prison fellowship seminar. And while Lucky didn't attend, he was curious about what was going on. Lucky began to find reasons to say hello to the chaplain. One day he needed a card. Another day he needed to make a phone call—and he wasn't as anxious to leave as he might previously have been. Lucky became like a coyote circling a bonfire on which a rabbit was cooking. Sniffing. Smelling something. Wondering. One of the Holy Spirit's most effective hooks is curiosity, which asks, "Why are you doing this?" "What is this all about?"

To make a long story short, we held a week of religious emphasis—you couldn't call them revivals, but we had religious emphasis. I did my own preaching. After all, this was my fellowship. This was my congregation. I was their pastor. At the last service on the last night of the week, someone said to me, "You're not going to believe it, but Lucky is here."

As we finished that service, I gave an invitation. I have no compunction about giving invitations to come to Christ. It's a voluntary thing. The doors are open. You come, you take what you want. You can leave without saying or doing anything, or you can make your feelings known.

I was about to close that session, saying, "Let's bow for prayer." I bowed my head, and I felt like the world had fallen on me. But what I really had on my shoulders was a sobbing, brokenhearted Lucky who could not speak, but whose tears said it all. It was almost as if all that bitterness, that anger, that resentment puddled out on the floor. Then he walked away.

So do you know why my impromptu committee was telling me I had to do something about Lucky—why I had better protect him? It seems he was down in the cellhouse holding prayer meetings in his cell! People who had always known him as a standup convict now were scared that he had really lost it. And if you know anything about prison populations you know that change is a sign or signal of something bad—but not in this instance. You know what I said to this group? I said, "Praise God."

Who can argue with a changed life? I say that my experience and your experience does not have to bow its knee to any logic or discipline because, after all, it's an honest experience. I don't have to give a logical defense of what I've experienced in my soul, and neither did Lucky.

Our most valid response to religious diversity, in other words, is simply to be who we are. I claim my heritage as a Christian minister and say clearly and openly, "This is who I am. This is what I'm about." I don't have to overcome other faiths if I have the ability to live and demonstrate my own.

The Practical Implications

What does all this mean in practical terms? First of all, I believe it means meeting people where they are without condemning them. That's exactly what Jesus did when he met the Samaritan woman at Jacob's well. Jesus, weary from his journey, was sitting by the well when the woman came to draw water:

Jesus said to her, "Give Me a drink." For His disciples had gone away into the city to buy food. The Samaritan woman therefore said to Him, "How is it that You, being a Jew, ask me for a drink since I am a Samaritan woman?" (For Jews have no dealing with Samaritans.)

Oh, what history has done to us! If we are Christians, we can't talk to those who aren't. If we are Baptists, we can't talk to Catholics. How unfortunate!

Jesus answered and said to her, "If you knew the gift of God and who it is who says to you, 'Give Me a drink,' you would have asked Him, and He would have given you living water."(John 4:7–10)

Jesus met that Samaritan woman where she was, as she was. Instead of condemning her or arguing with her, he paid attention to her needs and offered her what he had to give.

And that's how I believe we are to meet people from different religious backgrounds. In fact, I think one of the cruelest things we can do is to expect people to make a decision for Christ before they know who Christ is or before they have met a Christian.

Next, I believe our response to diversity means winning a hearing for the gospel by serving others. Once we say, "This is who I am" and "This is who you are," we say, "How can I help you?"— and mean it!

Jim Voss is a man who has had a powerful influence on me. Jim, who was converted at a Billy Graham crusade, is an electronic genius. Before his conversion, he had worked out a system to get East Coast racing results to Las Vegas ahead of the regular wire report. With his help, people could go in before they closed off the betting on a particular day and put money on the horse they already knew had won.

Jim left that scene when he came to Christ and began working with youth gangs on the city streets. And he has told me that his most effective tool is the ability to win a hearing for the gospel, to earn the right to share by what he does to help. Our response to diversity means winning a hearing for the gospel by reaching out to help people, to serve them.

A New Freedom

Unfortunately, the church has not always taken that approach. The Western world, which is primarily identified with the Christian faith, is still reaping the backlash of resentment left over from the Crusades, when medieval Christians set out to convert the Middle East by the sword and make a fortune in the meantime. (That tragic legacy is the reason we had to call our military chaplains "morale officers" during the Persian Gulf War.) And the history of Christianity contains many other examples of Christians who have tried to win a hearing through force and duress rather than service. As a result, we can expect a hostile response from time to time.

What can we do? Well, for one thing, we don't have to try to defend or rewrite history. What happened then wasn't our doing. Our only responsibility now is for who *we* are and how *we* respond and how *we* approach others. And we can go with this understanding: that whatever will stand the test of time and God's judgment will be born out of behavior that is consistent with the character of Christ. We can simply be Christian.

Do you know what that means to me? It means I am free not to manipulate for the master. I don't have to buttonhole and corral and argue with people. Logic doesn't win converts anyway; relationships are what attract people to Christ. And if other people believe differently and I have been obedient in ministering to them and sharing my faith with them, I can trust God to redeem the time I have spent with them.

When I resigned as general manager of the universe, I had so much more freedom than I ever had before. You see, I do not need to defend God. The living God, the Holy One, is able to defend himself. And interestingly enough, if I'm not sensitive when he's calling to another, if I'm not where I should be, waiting to be used by him, he'll raise somebody else up and still get the job done. The certainty of my faith frees me to serve all persons as if they matter to him also—because I believe they do. And that means I have the privilege of guarding the freedom of others to believe what they will. My defense is based on one simple but very important principle: that unless all are free to believe in any religion—Islam, Sikh, Hare Krishna, whatever—then none are free to believe. If I can watch the beliefs and customs of others being overridden and unregarded, if I fail to safeguard others' freedom to choose their religion, how can I expect to have my freedom guarded?

My response to diversity must be, then, that I claim my freedom to be fully and openly identified as a minister of Jesus Christ without apology. Then I am free to be me. I can be like the disciple Andrew and find a way to introduce the Greeks to Jesus. I can still see the little boy with three fishes in the midst of the great crowd because I have eyes for ministry. And I can still stand with Christ and watch what's going on in Gethsemane. I can have the sense of doing what I'm called to do without fear. When that happens, I can put into practice the characteristics of Christ. I can maintain his ethics in an ethical manner. I can be willing to do second-class jobs with a first-class spirit. And I can also provide equal everything to all faiths. Fairness will prevail, because my faith is not on the defensive. It is tried and proven and here to stay. I can honestly say that the integrity of my faith as a child of God is not compromised by this posture. What is the one characteristic we will not get anywhere in ministry without? Sincerity! If we are not the same on the outside as we are on the inside, we will have a problem. To minister effectively, we need openness and approachability without judgment or condemnation. Prisoners need to feel they are worthwhile and desirable to be with, and they measure that by how you respond to them.

Religious diversity is a fact—in our prisons as well as our society. However, diversity holds no fear for those who know who they are because they have discovered who God is. People who don't get so holy they forget who is can make a powerful impact for Christ's sake among the most diverse population.

6

Setting the Right Priorities

Bill Glass

Dynamic prison evangelist Bill Glass begins this chapter by calling our attention to the things that really count. He is troubled by the tendency of ministries to judge—both each other and those outside the ministry. This quarreling about minor matters of theology, practice, and personal preference creates doctrinal confusion for inmates. Mr. Glass's appeal is that we mainly be ministers of Christ's grace and reconciliation. He argues convincingly that church people often resemble Pharisees in arguing over small points and thereby missing the big picture. The big picture is practicing love, mercy, compassion, and forgiveness.

Jesus, according to Glass, was never predictable. He could use anyone and everyone in ministry. The lesson is obvious. There is room for everyone in prison ministry, regardless of educational background, denominational affiliation, or evangelism strategy, provided that all agree on the central issue of faith in Jesus for forgiveness of sins.

Bill Glass concludes his chapter by telling us to avoid pharasaism and to concentrate on the most important matter—to be ministers of the gospel and to bless, encourage, and edify one another and prisoners.

Our Lord's biggest battle during his earthly ministry was against legalism. Again and again, he confronted those who insisted on making that which was unimportant, important and that which was trivial, pivotal. Not surprisingly, his most committed enemies were the Pharisees, the religious group who made legalism and judgmentalism part of the language.

The apostle Paul battled against legalism, too. In Colossians 2, he asked how Christians could get so involved in trivial matters when so many important things need our attention. And that argument is the whole burden of Romans 14 as well. In this chapter, written in response to quibbles over dietary practices, he warns the Romans not to dispute over trivial, "doubtful things" (v. 1 NKJV).

That advice is for us, too, of course. God is in charge, and it is not our place to judge. Instead, we must immerse ourselves in matters that really count—loving, edifying, and encouraging one another. We are to be ministers of grace and reconciliation. The thrust of our lives must be in those areas, not in passing judgment on what others say or do.

We are always wrong when we judge! Christ gave great weight to this in the Sermon on the Mount. "Do not judge," he said, "or you too will be judged" (Matt. 7:1). And Paul elaborated on that message, saying, in effect, "Concerning areas that are not clear, just *shut up!*" Where the Bible speaks clearly we must listen and obey. But we are not to go around judging our brothers or sisters.

Not Just about Meat

The first four verses of Romans 14 tells us to accept others and let them be what God would have them be. We are not to impress our convictions on others. In this particular passage, the big controversy concerned eating meat that some said had been offered to idols. Some Jews said yes, it had been offered to idols, but it was still good meat. Others said that offering it to idols had contaminated it. But Paul made it clear that the big issue wasn't really eating meat. The real issue was personal convictions—and acting toward one another in love.

Most of us would agree that it is stupid to fight over eating meat. But what about going to movies, using cosmetics, wearing jewelry, playing cards, smoking, drinking, having too little or too much money, speaking in tongues, swimming in mixed company, wearing (or not wearing) certain clothes? The Scripture says very little about these things—unless you give some verses serious stretch marks.

So Paul's argument holds for these issues, too. If God leads me to do or not do some of these things, fine, but I must not apply my conviction to you. And if from the pulpit I make a statement that is clearly scriptural, not just a matter of taste, and you feel it applies to you, great. But you get into problems when you start applying it to other people directly—especially if it involves one of those legalistic ideas that we have incorporated and elevated to scriptural weight.

A Matter of Shame

We Christians are such shamers. We often say (or think), "You should be ashamed of yourself." While we were in Russia, we visited First Baptist Church of Moscow. A member of our team placed his Bible on the floor at church and a church member glared at him, as though he had committed some great sin. She didn't say anything, but her look was one of, "Shame on you! You should know better than to treat the Word of God like that!" We shame people for divorce, for marrying and for not marrying, for not having enough money or having too much, for sickness, for depression, for having too much fun, or for listening to Christian rock music.

We were conducting a citywide crusade in Corvallis, Oregon. On Wednesday night, we had a wild rock band. I didn't like the music very much. But five thousand kids came to hear the music, and hundreds of them trusted the Lord. A vocal few modern Pharisees in that town were critical of that "worldly" music. They were really objecting to the beat; the words were distinctively Christian. But I was saying, "Praise the Lord, if it draws the non-Christians." (You may say that it was the beat that was so sinful. Where do you find that in the Bible?)

I read about a German Lutheran convention for ministers where they served beer. All the Lutheran ministers drank beer.

But no one there smoked. If someone lit up a cigarette, he or she would have been considered a great sinner.

In Romans 14:3, the Scripture says, "Let not him who eats despise him who does not eat" (NKJV). A better translation is, "Do not treat him as nothing." When we honor someone, we give them weight; we tell them and show them they are important. When we regard them as nothing, we tell them they are lightweight. We must accept others as being valuable by taking them seriously. Don't shoot down their ideas. Don't shame them, even if you disagree with them.

One skeptic said, "Christians are the most guilt-ridden people I know." And one of the reasons we are so guilt-ridden is that we are such shamers. We shame others for not only sin, but for non-scriptural preferences.

Here's an example. I don't really like cigarette smoke. It irritates me. It is my preference not to smoke. But I can't find anything about smoking in the Bible.

Well, you may say, the Bible says the body is the temple of the Holy Spirit. But don't put stretch marks all over that verse. Perhaps it is true that I should not smoke because my body is the temple of the Holy Spirit. But that is open to question—a matter of personal conviction. It is a "doubtful thing." And Romans tells us directly not to dispute over doubtful things.

In our prison ministry, we had ten or fifteen prison counselors who smoked. And they were highly effective witnesses. They would go and smoke a cigarette with inmates and win them to the Lord in nothing flat. But a few of our other counselors—modern Pharisees—just needled those guys to death about their smoking. The nonsmokers got what they wanted. The smokers don't come with us anymore. We lost some of our best counselors.

It's essential that we understand the burden of Scripture on behavioral issues.

First, *we must only elevate to conviction status an item or action that is clearly covered in Scripture.* For example, it is my conviction that I must be faithful to my wife, because the Bible says clearly that I must not commit adultery. But I must not elevate to conviction things that are not clearly covered—"doubtful things" like smoking.

And here's something else: even if we are convicted that an issue is scripturally right or wrong, *we must apply that conviction to our own lives and not to others.* We are not to judge or to use our convictions of right or wrong as weapons.

If I quote "Wives, submit to your husbands" (Eph. 5:22) to my wife, then I use the Scripture like a club. What I ought to do is apply "Husbands, love your wives, just as Christ loved the church and gave himself up for her" (v. 25). That is the one that applies to me. But for me to use the Scripture against her, to judge her by it, is hitting below the belt. It's not Christian. It's not right.

These principles hold even in cases of overt sin. Jesus made this clear when a woman was caught in the act of adultery and brought before him. There was no question that what she did was scripturally wrong. But Jesus said to her accusers, "If any of you is without sin, let him be the first to cast a stone at her" (John 8:7). We must take that lesson to heart. Even in an area that is clearly sinful, the Lord tells us not to throw stones. Not to judge.

But Why?

Why all this emphasis on not judging? First, whenever we start worrying about other people's wrongful actions, we tend to lose sight of our own. We become self-righteous, closed-minded. We also tend to get hung up on externals or trivialities, obsessed with measuring our own righteousness. Our priorities become skewed, and we lose track of the major, important doctrines.

Jesus hated legalism, judgmentalism, and he doubly disliked the superpious attitude. And that is exactly what he found in the Pharisees. To them the Lord leveled his harshest criticism. He said they looked good on the outside, but their insides were full of dead men's bones. He called them white sepulchers. Pretty powerful!

The Pharisees were very concerned about external things, like how their clothes looked. They wanted the right number of tassels on the fringe of their robes. They wanted to look right when they prayed in the middle of the street, so everybody could see them. They wanted to keep the Sabbath laws in all their minute detail. And they wanted to make sure that everybody else respected those externals as well.

That overemphasis on externals motivates many a modern Pharisee as well. Some get upset over whether a woman is wearing too much makeup, or whether a male is wearing an earring (and in which ear!), or whether someone is wearing his hair too short or too long.

People even get pharisaical over externals of the Christian life. I asked one pastor if one of his members was a committed Christian. He replied, "Oh, yes, he is a three-service Christian. He comes to church three times a week. He is a great Christian." And even in our own group, I have heard counselors get upset because they did not see many decisions or brag because they had many decisions—even though the person who did not get many decisions might have been a more effective witness in the long run.

And just in case you're feeling judgmental about "those Pharisees" about now, remember that there is a little bit of the "whited sepulcher syndrome" in all of us. In fact, if I point a finger at them or at you, I have to point a thumb back at me. I, too, have become Mr. Pharisee all too often.

But there's another reason the Bible is so emphatic in telling us not to judge. Romans 14:9–12 says that we shouldn't judge because we are not qualified to judge. We are not qualified to judge for a lot of reasons. We don't know all the facts. We can't be totally objective and see the big picture. We have blind spots and are imperfect and inconsistent ourselves.

I recently read about a survey done in the state of Connecticut. Thousands of people signed a petition saying they were against reckless driving. More officers were hired to enforce the law. And the first five people stopped for reckless driving had signed the petition against reckless driving earlier that day! They applied it to others, but not to themselves.

When we judge others, we are playing God, usurping his position, telling him how to do what he does best. And that's the height of arrogance!

In creation, God had a sense of humor. He made a buzzard and a butterfly, a zinnia and an orchid, a minnow and a shark. He loved and used Rahab the whore and Esther the queen. He made Amos, the fig-picker turned prophet, and Stephen, the deacon turned martyr. Predictability is really boring, and our Lord has seldom done the expected. He used a man who had committed adultery and murder to become one of the great saints of all times, the most prominent person in the Old Testament—David. He used a multiple murderer to become a great evangelist in the New Testament—Paul.

God knows what he is doing. And he says, "Let the wheat and the tares grow up together. In the end, I will decide who the real wheat is and who the weeds are. In the meantime, stay out of my business." In other words, humans don't function well as judges.

Don't Avoid the Lost

Modern Pharisees use the word *separation* a lot. They talk about "not being of the world." But what many of them mean by separation is isolation. They fear contamination by the outside world.

That is the problem with many of our Christian schools. Now, I am not against Christian education. I am all for it, as long as we don't put our kids in a Christian school to protect them rather than prepare them. But Christ never called us to hide ourselves away. We are not to be "of the world," but we are definitely to be *in* it. We are not to avoid the lost, but to seek the lost!

I heard about a little boy who ran into the living room, dangling a very dead mouse by the tail. "I killed a mouse! I killed a mouse!" he yelled. He didn't realize the pastor was visiting his mother. He said, "I beat the mouse in the head with a baseball bat. I jumped up and down on top of him. I beat him with a rock." Then he saw the minister was there, so he said, "And then he went home to be with the Lord." It's too bad that people think they have to talk with a holy tone when they get around a pastor.

Paul was the reverse. Paul said he wanted to become "all things to all men" so that he might, by all means, win some. Take your cue from Paul. Adapt yourself to your audience. Talk in his language. Don't sacrifice that which is clearly your valid biblical conviction, but start with people where they are. If they are interested in sports, start with sports. If they are interested in music, start with music. Then move them to the Lord. Seek to be extremely spiritual, but perfectly natural.

In Luke 5:30, the Pharisees attacked Jesus for eating with the publicans, the tax collectors. They assumed that anyone who ate with tax collectors was wicked. But Christ answered that he spent his time with sinners because sinners were the ones who needed him. And we, too, are called to spend time with those who need Christ—whether we approve of their actions or not.

What would be the modern equivalent of publicans—the group most hated and feared? For many of us, especially men, homosexuals would be the most repulsive group we could think of. If we can love and have compassion toward the homosexual, then we can love anyone. So we Christians must not put homosexuals down, shame them or deride them, even when talking among ourselves. Even among prison workers, I have heard snide remarks about homosexuals. This is not of God!

I am not saying homosexuality isn't a sin. The Bible clearly states that it is. But take a look at 1 Corinthians 6:9–11, which lists every conceivable sin, including homosexuality. It says clearly, "And that is what some of you were." The early church was built from all types of sinful people. And so is the church today.

A Christian leader recently said, "We do real well with those who are just like us. But we don't do well with those who are richer and smarter, or dumber and poorer than us." He said we should reach out to those who are richer and smarter and those who are dumber and poorer because they too need the Lord.

I will broaden his statement. We need to reach out to those who are more sinful than we are and even those who are more self-righteous than we are. We should reach out to those who are different than we are—the homosexual, the drunkard, the drug addict. But we can't reach out to them effectively if we make fun of them, even out of their presence.

The Pharisees said Christ was not really a true prophet because he ate with the tax collectors. They were looking at an entire group and saying they are inferior. And that was a sin! It is sin to look at all of any group and say they are beyond help.

Remember, the verse says, "Such were some of you." Some of you were homosexuals, or tax collectors, but you have been washed and changed. That is the emphasis of the New Testament.

That doesn't mean that we have to go out and party with those whose actions we feel are wrong. But we could treat them with respect. We could invite them over to our house for supper. We could befriend them.

One ten-year-old boy in a citywide crusade in New Jersey got concerned about his friends and invited them to a crusade service. They wouldn't come. So he asked them to come over for hot dogs and they came, knowing they were going to the service after hot dogs. Ten kids came with him, and four came to the Lord. He befriended those in the neighborhood who weren't Christians. How long has it been since you had someone who wasn't a Christian over to your house for supper?

I have found that after two years, most new Christians are pretty well neutralized as witnesses. That is because we don't move in non-Christian circles anymore. All we do is duck between Christian groups, and therefore we don't have any influence over the lost.

I like to speak to the group called "Gathering of Men." They operate on this principle: Find a man who isn't a Christian and bring him with you to breakfast, we can then win him to the Lord. They are reaching out beyond their own little group.

If you say, "I do not like the sound of this," then you don't like the sound of "Go ye therefore into all the world and tell them of me." You don't like the sound of Scripture. The New Testament Christian leaders were given to hospitality. Why? In order to win the lost world around them.

Why does our ministry bring in all athletes from all over America at great expense for our prison visits? Because, you see, inmates like sports. You may say, "Why don't you let the Lord draw them?" Paul said to become all things to all men that you might by all means win some.

We went to Visalia, California, and tried to get a certain church to cooperate in our citywide crusade. They would not cooperate because they were an independent, fundamental, premillenial, separated Baptist church. They don't cooperate with anybody on anything. But one of their members, Bill Pruitt, came to the crusade, became very involved, and then followed by coming to our prison ministry as a counselor. He was very excited about our prison ministry and, after being a counselor for several years, he became a volunteer coordinator and state director for California. He tried to get members of his church to come with him, but they wouldn't come. They wouldn't come because they were an independent, fundamental, premillenial, separated Baptist church.

He finally did get one guy to come, who got very excited. He went back and got some others. Finally, thirty-one members of that church came, and the last guy to come was the pastor. He said, "I did a survey and discovered that all but one of the people who came and served as counselors in the prisons won someone on the streets of Visalia within a month of the time they served in prison."

I told Tim LaHaye this story and he said, "That which you repeat under pressure tends to groove itself into permanence." We repeat the plan of salvation under pressure over and over again in prison, and when we went back to our hometown, we naturally share with those at home. We went back to Visalia a couple of years ago, and this church was the leading church in that city-wide crusade. I commended that pastor, because it is tough in his group to break out of that pharisaism that says we don't cooperate with anybody because they "eat with publicans." It's the mindset that says, he may be all right himself, but those people he socialized with will corrupt him. Or you may preach the gospel, but some of the cooperating churches belong to the National Council of Churches. To his great credit, this pastor helped us in spite of the tremendous pressure put on him.

A Wise Liberty

In Christ, the behavioral guidelines are simple. If something is clearly forbidden or discouraged in Scripture, we should avoid it. But even if we sin, we can be made right with God through confessing our sin and asking for forgiveness in Jesus' name.

If something is not clearly covered in Scripture, we are free to follow our own conviction and the Holy Spirit's guidance—but not to impose our conviction on others. And even if a certain action is clearly forbidden in Scripture, it's not up to us to judge or convict others. That's God's job. Our job is to keep our eyes on the essentials of the gospel and reach out in love to others—even to those whose actions we deplore.

Life in Christ, then, is a lifestyle of liberty. When we come to him, we are freed from the burden of having to keep a long set of rules and regulations. We are freed from our guilt, freed from our shame, free to follow our own convictions.

However, it is possible for us to misuse our liberty to our own or someone else's detriment. That's why Romans 14:19–22 tells us that we should express our liberty wisely. Even if we are free to do something, we should refrain if our doing it would hurt someone else. Pharisees have always been hard to live with. Christ couldn't abide them, and I don't like myself or others when we act like them. When we have love and joy and peace, people look forward to seeing us because they know we will not judge them, that we leave convicting to the Lord. Our job is to bless, encourage, and edify.

That is the basis of our evangelism to prisoners–to bless them, not condemn them; to encourage them, not judge them; to minister to prisoners out of a posture of humility rather than one of superiority.

Part 4

Seeking Justice

Introduction

Bill Glass once told me that prisoners standing before a sentencing judge often cry out for *justice* when they really mean *mercy*. "If we really got what we deserve," Bill commented, "then we are all in trouble." And Bill is right, of course. It is through the sacrifice of Jesus Christ that we can come before God's throne and find mercy for our numerous offenses instead of true justice for our sins.

But even in his great mercy, God remains a God of justice! He is a God who proclaims, through the prophets,

> Let justice run on like a river,
>   righteousness like a never-failing stream. (Amos 5:24)

And he tells us through Scripture that justice should be our concern as well.

But it's important to remember that the scriptural view of justice embraces far more than just enforcing the law and punishing lawbreakers. In the Bible, justice means righting wrongs, restoring relationships, healing wounds. As Richard Halverson, the chaplain of the United States Senate, points out, "Justice and righteousness come from the same root. To be just is to be righteous; to be righteous is to be just."

How do we help bring God's kind of justice about? The answer is really simple: by reflecting on God's Word and using the principles he gave us.

What are those principles? Jesus summed them up concisely: to love God with our whole hearts and minds and to love our neighbors as ourselves (Matt. 22:37–39). And in Matthew 25, which describes the Last Judgment, he made it clear that we cannot have a vertical relationship with God without a horizontal relationship with our brothers and sisters, especially those weakest and hurting: "And the King will reply, 'I tell you the truth, whatever you did for one of the least of these brothers of mine, you did for me" (Matt. 25:40).

According to this passage and others, God takes it *personally* when we ignore the hurts and needs of those around us. And this applies especially to those most abused and rejected by society: the poor, the hungry, the widowed . . . and the prisoners.

A Voice for Justice

John Perkins is a man with a unique message for our culture and for prison ministry. An African American, born the son of sharecroppers and brought up in the segregated deep South, he understands the thirst for justice in a personal way—and his has been a prophetic voice calling the American church to work for justice. Rightfully, he has gained the attention of the evangelical church nationwide for his work among the poor in Mississippi and his Center of Reconciliation in Pasadena, California. I have been inspired and renewed by Dr. Perkins's teachings, especially in those times we have been together personally.

Dr. Perkins states unequivocally that

> we cannot talk about preaching the gospel without really seeing *justice* as the main element. Motivation for God's redemption was his own justice and holiness and righteousness. Clearly to love God with your whole heart is to also love your neighbor. In that is justice.[1]

Dr. Perkins has taken a special interest in the ministry to prisoners, especially because the African-American population has been so affected by America's criminal justice system. (More than 25 percent of all young black males in our country are incarcerat-

---

1. Excerpts from speeches given by Dr. Perkins at Wheaton College.

ed or on probation or parole.) On several occasions Dr. Perkins has spoken at Wheaton College about prison ministry, which he sees as a close-to-home beginning point for the Great Commission:

> The purpose of the incoming of the Holy Spirit in our lives is to have the power to witness effectively for him in Jerusalem, Judea, Samaria, and the uttermost parts of the world. . . . But, before I run off to the ends of the world, the gospel must work in Samaria, and it must work across cultures, across social and economic barriers.

Dr. Perkins has advocated two principles for effective prison ministry: (1) indigenous leadership development, and (2) Christian community development. Clearly, our crime and our criminals come from a community and will go back to that community after their imprisonment. That is why he advocates developing the local Christian community to take care of its own wounded. Aftercare, after all, is about the *quality* of the community where the offenders are returning. That is why Dr. Perkins calls for indigenous leadership development. Prison ministry cannot depend on white suburbanites to infiltrate the minority neighborhoods of an urban culture.

But that does *not* mean that churches should confine their ministry efforts to those who are like them. To the contrary, Perkins demonstrates that many of us must reach beyond our evangelical culture and our heritage to see justice established. Too often, he charges, "We are trying to bring credibility to the tradition that we have shaped. Let's go back instead to the teachings of Jesus and to the mind of Christ. Not everything the founding fathers taught was good, especially slavery."

Perkins says, "The more and more we are like Jesus, the more we will want to have a long relationship with each other. I think we have gone to extremes with individualism. We think we can achieve more individually than we can achieve as the body of Christ, but in prison ministry, as in the church, we need to work together."

Perkins continues,

> Jesus' life was in absolute accord with what was written about him in the Old Testament. The prophets said clearly that we would

know the Messiah by where he would give his major attention. He was going to give his major attention to the poor and to the broken in the world. That was going to be his identity. And so Jesus authenticated himself, so the world would know he was the Messiah. He went out to the truly dejected and rejected. Therefore going to prison and going to the poor is our identity as followers of Christ. There is no option. That is our identity!

If we are to bring justice to a system riddled with inequity and prejudice, Dr. Perkins suggests that the church remember its own identity and adjust its priorities accordingly. He charges,

> The church has become basically a middle-class institution. We have black churches and white churches. And most of the resources of the white church are being used on themselves. The church has become an extension of individualism, selfishness, and greed. And that's what makes prosperity Christianity so popular— because it fits into our culture; it fits into what the church has taught us. By this we have lost our identity, and it is difficult for the world to believe in us.
>
> We need to authenticate our faith. We need to let people know we are Christians by following the teachings of Jesus: going to the poor, going to the broken, and going to the prisons. The Messiah gave his attention to the people society had rejected. And our credibility is in our concern for the poor. . . . As followers of Christ, we are to be light, especially to those people who are in darkness, to those people who live in the region of the shadow of death.

I am impressed by Dr. Perkins's impassioned plea that the church not be a self-serving institution. And I agree that in some ways we have lost our identity as ministers to the outcast, poor, and needy. To follow our Lord, we must go to the region of the shadow of death—which very much includes jails and prisons of America. These are in many ways the people who need us—and God's kind of justice—the most. Many prisoners are socially damaged. They have been processed through a system that is riddled with racism and bigotry. In this witness, the gospel will be the visible demonstration of God's love to the poor and to the prisoners.

Making the System More Just

Practically speaking, how do we ensure justice in a system administered by men and women who are just as weak and as sinful as those who are adjudicated?

To begin with, we must have realistic expectations for the system. There is simply no perfect justice in this world. However, we can hope for, and certainly work toward, a system that is more fair and impartial and that comes closer to establishing righteousness. This does not happen by chance. Citizens and particularly the church, the body of Christ, must be the watchdogs of justice on multiple levels.

Justice that is righteous and fair must be a priority at every stage of encounter between the offender and the system, from arrest to incarceration. I believe we should have two unimpeachable standards:

The system must be as free from bias and racial prejudice as possible.

What is done to the offender at each level must not exceed what the situation necessitates.

Justice at the Point of Arrest

At the point of arrest, I believe the police should use discretion in charging crimes. Whenever possible, and especially in domestic situations, mediation and conflict resolution should be considered an option. This question should be asked: Will the filing of a complaint and a subsequent court procedure help this situation by protecting individuals and society, or will it exacerbate the problem and unduly complicate the lives of people who are already hurting?

Many cases would not result in a complaint if officers used more discretion and discernment. For example, in cases of shoplifting, public embarrassment, and petty crimes by children, involving parents in these situations is usually sufficient to turn around behaviors—and protracted court procedures could result in labeling the child and perhaps initiating a self-fulfilling prophecy.

Arrest should never be considered a mandatory response to disturbance. Instead, police officers should be trained and encouraged to lay aside emotional bias and to make decisions at the point of arrest that result in the greater good.

Even when arrest is necessary, undue force should be avoided. Rough treatment and verbal abuse are totally unacceptable in most instances, especially in situations of nonviolent crime. Many citizens have known the experience of being intimidated or bullied by abusive officers during a routine traffic stop. Others have been harassed or singled out by race or ethnic group. These abuses of authority and power should not be tolerated by our society.

In Milwaukee, the summer of 1991, neighbors of Jeffrey Dahmer repeatedly called police regarding his suspicious activities. In his apartment, officers failed to investigate peculiar odors and returned a naked and bleeding fourteen-year-old victim to Dahmer. After the police left, the young man was murdered. Dahmer's African-America neighbors made subsequent calls to police, but were ignored. Many suspect that the police were not responsive because of the racial makeup of the neighborhood. I believe the subsequent suspension of the officers involved was fully justified.

The nation was shocked by the video documentation of the severe beating of Rodney King by Los Angeles police during his arrest in 1990. But the only truly unusual fact about that beating was that it was documented. In fact, L.A. police chief Daryl Gates had once said, "Casual, occasional marijuana users ought to be taken out and shot." What message did such a comment send to his police?[2]

The motto of the Los Angeles Police Department is "To protect and to serve." We assume this means to *protect* the community. But it should also mean protecting the rights of individual citizens—including those who are arrested. To *serve* should mean the interest of society—which again comes back to fair and just administration of police duties.

Subsequent to the videotaped beating of the motorist, it was discovered that many taped radio transmissions between patrol

---

2. *Los Angeles Times*, October 1991.

cars in L.A. included such phrases as "Capture him, beat him, and treat him like dirt." Another radio transmission said,

> They give me a stick.
> They give me a gun.
> They pay me 30 G's to have some fun.

This comes from the highest paid police force in America. Entry-level base pay in Los Angeles ranges from thirty-two to thirty-four thousand dollars, higher than any other city and any federal agency, including the FBI and the DEA. Even in a lower-paid force, however, such lack of professionalism—not to mention lack of compassion—is inexcusable.

Los Angeles is not the only city that has witnessed convoluted justice in its police force. Patterns of abuse in Chicago have been known for years. Many arrested have been beaten. Gang members have been dropped off in rival gang territories with a loudspeaker proclamation from the squad car, insuring that the individual would be more seriously harmed.

At a 1991 convention, Chicago Police Commissioner Leroy Martin recommended suspending parts of the United States Constitution in order to fight crime. For instance, he suggested suspending the guarantees against unreasonable searches so that police would have the power to investigate without search warrants. During a radio show, Commissioner Martin was informed that Adolf Hitler had policies in Nazi Germany that began with similar constitutional suspensions. Martin responded, "And they had a very low crime rate then." He was actually suggesting that a police state with unlimited police power is better for our society!

Amnesty International usually probes the violations of human rights in third-world countries. According to the *Chicago Tribune*, August 1991, it began investigating torture at the hands of Chicago police. Andrew Wilson was killed by two police officers in 1982 when he was brought to the Pullman area station on suspicion of killing a police officer. Before his death, he was tortured, given electric shocks through wires clipped to his ears. In 1987, the Illinois Supreme Court ruled that Wilson's confession had been coerced as a result of the torture. The court also found that the police had a policy of allowing officers to torture suspected "cop killers." No officers ever came to trial.

Unfortunately, a series of recent laws and court decisions have had the affect of making such abuse of authority even more likely. A House-approved anticrime bill passed in October 1991 states that as long as arresting officers acted "in good faith," they could seize evidence without a warrant. The bill was not passed by the Senate, but similar legislation is pending. About the same time, a United States Supreme Court decision made it easier for the police to search houses for drugs and to open and examine suitcases and paper bags they find in trunks of cars and in buses. The court also allowed prosecutors to use coerced confessions as evidence against defendants.

The Supreme Court justices also substantially weakened the 1983 decision that interpreted the Eighth Amendment to the Constitution, which prohibits cruel and unusual punishment. A Michigan law requiring a life sentence for the possession of 672 grams of cocaine was upheld as not unusual, not cruel, and not unconstitutional. The majority opinion was written by Justice Antonin Scalia. This may be an indication of a trend toward the reduction of individual rights and a greater potential for harming the innocent.

All this is not to say that the majority of police officers are brutal or that the use of force in an arrest or other law-enforcement situation is always wrong. There are obvious situations when the life of an officer is jeopardized and self-defense measures are required. Still, justice cannot be served when arresting officers and their superiors consider themselves the jury, judge, and in some cases the executioner.

Prosecuting for Justice

It is the duty of the attorneys who prosecute a crime on behalf of the people to seek a conviction. However, the same standards of not exceeding what the situation dictates that apply to arresting officers should apply also to prosecutors. For instance, when evidence is weak or there is a considerable doubt as to the guilt of an offender, the case should not be prosecuted. Often there are political motives for prosecuting weak cases when there is public outcry and no other suspects.

Understandably, the prosecutor enhances his career with a long record of successful convictions. By its nature, the role combines the profession of jurisprudence with politics. But if justice is to be served, political demands must be balanced with other considerations. The prosecutor should ask himself or herself, will this conviction result in a more complicated situation for the individual? Will prison make the offender worse? Will incarceration devastate employment, stability, and family? Is there an acceptable alternative to trial?

It's important to remember that even if an individual is found innocent, he or she is nonetheless damaged. In some cases it has cost great sums of money to mount an adequate defense. (Even when the public defender is used, the taxpayer pays!) The press too often implies guilt as they cover trials, adversely affecting reputations, another form of harm.

The compiling of multiple offenses sometimes has the effect of overkill. As an example, when somebody commits a burglary, certain other charges are implicit: possession of burglary tools, criminal damage to property, trespassing, possession of stolen property, and so on. As the charges mount, if there is a conviction on each of them, then the length of sentence for a single crime becomes greater. Obviously, one cannot commit a burglary without simultaneously trespassing on private property!

In the case of an habitual burglar, the combining of multiple offenses insures that the offender will be out of circulation for some time. And the multiple offenses can also be a bargaining tool in a plea reduction that saves the court considerable money. But multiple counts can also make a first time or youthful offender look like public-enemy number one in the media and court records. This tool of the court system should be used very carefully.

It ought to be obvious that prosecutors should not pander to public opinion for political reasons or deliberately play on juror prejudices to obtain convictions. The same would apply to the defense, of course. Unfortunately, such manipulation is often considered "part of the game."

Judges always ask potential jurors if they believe they can be fair and free of bias. I've been perplexed by the number of prospective jurors I have heard say they will act completely free of any prejudice or bias. Who is so objective and free of bias?

A sociological study in Minnesota in the early eighties indicated that jurors base their decisions not on facts presented in the court, but on more subtle influences such as the appearance of the defendant (length of hair, clothes, and facial expressions). The study indicated that jurors were more likely to find guilt if the offender was out of work, smoked, or did not dress well. Conversely, a juror was less likely to find guilt if the accused was a professional—well dressed, educated, articulate, and with a good reputation in the community. All of this simply indicates that the rich and those with influential friends will not find the same kind of justice before the bar as the poor and disenfranchised. To be fair in prosecution, we must try to overcome these inequities, not cash in on them!

Fair Judgment

The ultimate power of a judge lies in his or her ability to do something to the convicted criminal that harms him or her. The judge imposes a penalty, withdraws the privilege of a driver's license, takes away freedom through incarceration, or even takes away life by execution. Unfortunately, that power can be abused, and such abuse gets in the way of justice.

I have observed that many judges get caught in power plays in the courtroom. One particular judge I worked with would threaten a man for getting behind in child-support payments. Obviously the court had jurisdiction and authority in the case. But from the beginning, the judge would say, "Bring your toothbrush next time if you aren't caught up."

The toothbrush reference clearly represented a threat to send the man to jail. At the next appearance, if the man was still behind in his payments, the judge was not about to back down. Promptly the bailiff handcuffed the man and took him off to jail. The consequences, however, went far beyond the judge proving that he had power and was serious. The jailed man lost his job and thereby any potential of making any future child-support payments. The child and mother went from partial payments to no payments at all. Once released from jail, the man, having been terminated by his employer, was not eligible for unemployment benefits and had to seek aid from the welfare system. He became depressed. A drinking problem resulted in a violation of his probation and more jail time. Eventually his life disintegrated and he turned to more serious crime. He never did catch up with his child support. What was accomplished?

Judges who want to be truly fair must ask themselves if, overall, they are making situations better or creating bigger problems both for the individuals involved and for society in general.

Fairness in judging also involves serious consideration of alternative forms of punishment. As we have seen, there are many punishments for nonviolent offenders that can reduce the terrible overcrowding in our prison systems, while keeping families intact and letting offenders continue their gainful employment. In nonviolent cases, judges should be open to using volunteers as community mediators.

For adjudication to be fair financially, indigent individuals should receive the same defense as rich ones. This does not happen. Fairness also implies swifter justice. Long delays and continuances can drag out cases for months and years, disrupting lives. A suspect unable to pay bond, even if innocent, sits in jail during these waiting periods.

Finally, judges should be aware that the longer a person's sentence, the more his or her behavior tends to worsen. With this in mind, judges should choose incarceration only as a last resort.

Incarceration—A Scarce Resource

For incarceration to be utilized fairly, it should be considered a scarce resource. As we have seen, the loss of freedom should be used only when the protection of society is paramount. For example, dangerous and violent offenders usually need to be segregated from society. Even then, however, we must keep in mind that the punishment involved is loss of freedom, not the myriad abuses that sometimes come with it.

Correctional systems must work harder to reduce overcrowding that often leads to physical and sexual abuse. That should not be considered part of the punishment, especially for a nonviolent offender. By reducing the population of prisons from thousands to hundreds of inmates, we can return to a one inmate, one cell principle. This allows all inmates a modicum of human dignity and spares inmates from the influence of more corrupt or dangerous cellmates.

Prisons must also work more diligently at hiring professional correctional officers who can protect against abuse and help stamp out gang infiltration. It goes without saying, of course, that abuse by corrections personnel themselves should not be tolerated.

It is a tragedy that most prisoners can obtain most drugs during their incarceration. Drug and alcohol abuse is often a part of the offender's past lifestyle and a major contributor to the crime that brought him or her to prison. (More than 80 percent of offenders are dependent on drugs or alcohol at the time of arrest.) Continuing access to illegal substances can only lead to the further disintegration of the individual's personality and behavior.

Most prison environments are predatory and perverse. In 1990 the *New York Times* reported that the Iowa Men's Reformatory, which houses nine hundred convicted men, features an official pornographic reading room. Federal District Judge Harold Vietor ruled that prisoners should be entitled to the same magazines that are available to other Iowans. This kind of reasoning is ludicrous. Child molesters, rapists, and other sexual offenders certainly do not need pornographic magazines. Allowing these people access to such material is as injurious as giving the alcoholic or drug addict unlimited access to illegal contraband. It certainly does not promote justice.

As mental-health services and community psychiatric facilities have been downsized or eliminated, prisons have increasingly become dumping grounds for the mentally ill. I have personally observed many individuals with obvious symptoms of mental illness being housed in America's prisons. The sight of naked young men clawing at imaginary creatures and screaming has stayed vividly in my mind. Warehousing such unfortunate individuals in prisons where they cannot receive adequate care and where they are subject to abuse is a monumental injustice.

In 1991 the prison population of Indiana, like that in other states, was running 20 percent over capacity. In response, Commissioner of Corrections James Aiken devised a plan to predict the need for prison expansion. "People think prisoners come out of trees, but they don't," argued Aiken. "They come out of the second grade." The state of Indiana, therefore, will project the number of future cells needed by estimating the number of second graders in that state who are at "risk." Such a plan takes on an Orwellian overtone. Do we really think we can look at a seven-year-old and predict his future as an adult?

Even when imprisonment is necessary, there are several measures we need to take to make that time productive. This includes meaningful work. Prisoners need a strong work ethic. They need to develop practical job skills. In the past, the kind of work done in the prison did little to prepare offenders for realistic, gainful employment in society.

Through positive incentives, prisoners should be encouraged to continue their educations. Most prisoners read and write at a fourth-grade level. It is not uncommon for the majority of inmates in an institution to be high-school dropouts. We should encourage the attaining of high school equivalency degrees (GED) and encourage correspondence courses, including those on a college level.

Drug and alcohol treatment and education should be essential in prisons. So should adequate diagnosis and treatment for mental illness. And once again, alternatives to incarceration should be considered whenever possible. In all but the most extreme cases, justice is not served best by locking offenders up in our penal institutions.

Toward Higher Standards of Justice

Politicians often use inflammatory rhetoric about "getting tough on crime" to get the attention and the votes of a crime-weary public. The famous Willie Horton ads used in the 1988 presidential election are a case in point. These ads, which attacked Democratic candidate Michael Dukakis for paroling a prisoner who later returned to crime, deliberately pandered to everyone's worst fears and prejudices. They reinforced the popular but wrong conception that justice is best served by taking a hard line on offenders. Unfortunately, this attitude just leads to abuse and a worsening of the problems in our criminal justice system.

In place of the "get tough on crime" mindset, I propose that we need to rethink our concept of justice and pay attention to what methods truly further justice for victim, offender, and society.

And the impetus for this change must come from outside the criminal justice system.

Ralph Waldo Emerson was right when he said, "The field cannot well be seen from within the field." We cannot depend on the police, the judges, and the wardens to execute their duties and at the same time evaluate the system objectively. In part, that is a job for philosophers, sociologists, and theologians, who are better equipped to evaluate the ethics of our current system. But it is also a job for all of us—for us as a society and particularly us as Christians. We hold the ultimate responsibility for seeking true justice in our criminal justice system.

7

Cry for Justice, Hope for Shalom

James W. Skillen

Dr. James Skillen, a scholar who has studied justice issues extensively, begins his chapter by reviewing the experience of Job as compared with the righteousness of God. He concludes that God is in control even when we have our doubts, that good people suffer for a greater purpose.

This theme becomes Dr. Skillen's vehicle for discussion of the true nature of justice. He describes a self-righteous America more concerned with getting rid of lawbreakers than with seeking justice. The central feature of this chapter is that our popular concept of justice is too narrow. God doesn't just want the finding of guilt or innocence, release or punishment. God wants people to be reconciled. The church is to take seriously our civic responsibility of not ignoring the system but having an abiding desire to see real justice accomplished.

Another feature of this chapter is Dr. Skillen's portrayal of Jesus as the second Job—his suffering a far greater mystery than Job's. He concludes the chapter by stating that God is concerned about justice and that justice is best exemplified through Christ's kingdom and a ministry of reconciliation.

The Lord said to Job:
  "Will the one who contends with the Almighty correct
     him?
  Let him who accuses God answer him!"

Then Job answered the Lord:
  "I am unworthy—how can I reply to you?
     I put my hand over my mouth.
  I spoke once, but I have no answer—
     twice, but I will say no more."

Then the Lord spoke to Job out of the storm:
  "Brace yourself like a man;
     I will question you,
     and you shall answer me.
  Would you discredit my justice?
  Would you condemn me to justify yourself?"

                                                    (Job 40:1–8)

All evidence suggests that Job was a righteous man. His book begins with the disclosure that he was "blameless and upright; he feared God and shunned evil" (1:1). The Lord himself tells Satan about Job, "There is no one on earth like him; he is blameless and upright, a man who fears God and shuns evil" (1:8).

But Satan chides God: No wonder Job is righteous; look how well you treat him! Satan implies, in other words, that God's world is a sham, a mere pretense, an unjust fake, because Job's uprightness is purely external, not inherent in his character.

God responds to Satan by granting permission to put Job to the test. You may strip away everything he has, God tells Satan, but don't take his life. Let's see who is just and whether my creation is designed with integrity.

After finishing his destructive work, Satan remains unable to push Job to the cursing point. He cannot expose Job as a hypocrite. Thus, he is stymied in trying to prove that God and his world are a sham. Nevertheless, the awful test leaves Job with many questions. With or without the "help" of his advisers, Job wonders, above all, what it means to live a righteous life in a world where righteousness doesn't necessarily pay off. He doesn't give up on God, but he does wonder about God's way of running things.

Just that little bit of questioning, however, is enough to bring the Lord charging into the courtroom, where he addresses Job and his friends with the words that I quoted at the beginning of the chapter. God certifies to Job, with dramatic testimony, that he *does* know what he is doing. And Job is silenced. He stands helpless and undone before the mysterious and righteous God.

Too Little Justice

I begin with Job's experience because the largest and most important questions about justice confronting us today extend beyond human management of crimes and punishments. Even when the processes and penalties in our criminal justice system are "just," they constitute only one small part of the just ordering of this world. And when those processes and penalties turn out to be unjust, they merely deepen the question of ultimate justice.

Part of the difficulty America faces today is that too many of its citizens seem to be concerned more about getting rid of lawbreakers than about justice. They appear unaware that the proper aim of retribution against evil deeds is to restore order, to reconcile people to one another, to sustain a just society. Instead, they are preoccupied with punishing offenders so that they, who are righteous, can live in peace. And the more crime increases, the more mindless and expensive becomes their pursuit of ways to put criminals out of sight.

But what is just about spending an ever-increasing percentage of precious public resources on prisons that produce more criminals than they restore? What is just about penalizing criminals without reconciling them to their victims through various means of recompense? What is just about fining or locking up the few lawbreakers we can catch while remaining helpless to deal with those who get away? What is just about penalizing those thought to be offenders who are actually innocent?

"Oh," but you say, "no system is perfect. If we wait until perfect justice can be achieved before we deal with offenders, then crime will only grow worse. Better to have a little justice than none at all. We know that some deeds are wrong and should be punished. If we can catch the offender, then, we ought to prosecute. That may not achieve very much justice, but every little bit helps."

Now, don't get me wrong. My message to you is *not* to disparage small bits of retributive justice as worthless or to suggest that we ought to vote for the complete dismantling of all police forces and court systems. What I do want to say, however, is that too little justice exists in America today. And this is due in part to the fact that Americans, including Christians, operate with far too narrow a conception of justice.

The result is that we often don't hear the cry for justice from many who are suffering injustice. Moreover, when we who think of ourselves as law-abiding citizens suddenly become the victims of crime, we all too often shift dramatically from being naive supporters of the system to becoming cynically suspicious. If the system seems not to work very well because it doesn't do justice to us, we become outraged and alienated. Many victims, like most people behind bars, then give up hope of ever experiencing genuine shalom.

The story of Job, therefore, should grab our attention at regular intervals. On the surface, it seems obvious that Job was the innocent victim of Satan's crimes. Job got caught in the war game that God and Satan were playing. He suffered grave injustice, it seems, and the logical conclusion is that someone should be punished—or at least called to account. Job has a right to be outraged. The system didn't work very well for him.

According to Job's story, however, the one we would have to charge and prosecute—at least as a coconspirator—is God. God, not Job, is guilty. But wait just a minute. Are we any more justified in reaching that conclusion than Job was? Do we stand in any position to pass judgment on God? Job may have suffered what seems to have been unjustified pain. But in the larger scheme of things, according to the story, God was proving that he is just and will reward his servants, including Job, even when all the odds seem stacked against them.

Asking the Deeper Questions

What Job's story demonstrates, I think, is that ultimate justice is not a matter of momentary incidents alone. True justice displays itself only through lifelong patterns of personal integrity, lifelong habits of walking with God, lifelong endurance in working to create and sustain public health and good order.

Furthermore, true justice cannot be understood apart from the continual exercise of suspicion about our own righteousness. It requires the popping of all balloons filled with self-righteous pretension by which we imagine that only "others" are a danger to society. Understanding and doing justice begins with the recognition that we are *all* guilty of evil and deserve God's punishment. Only God is just, and who can fathom his ways?

In America today the dominant attitude seems to be that the good guys are those who mind their own business and don't commit serious public offenses. Danger to society comes from "others." Of course the police can't catch all crooks. But as long as they catch enough of them to send out a warning signal, then we can accept our system as adequate and sufficient for this world. But what kind of society spawns as many lawbreakers and lawbenders as we now have in America—ranging from drug dealers to bank rip-off artists? As part of that society, surely we bear part of the blame.

Besides, don't we all bear some responsibility for promoting a just public order, not simply for minding our own business? Shouldn't we be seeking reconciliation between offender and victim and not simply incarcerating a host of criminals? Shouldn't citizens be held accountable for contributing to the positive well-being of society and not merely for staying out of trouble?

What is our ultimate civic aim anyway? Is it simply to hope against hope that we will be able to pass through this life without getting mugged? Is it to have enough freedom to pursue our own personal gain while the police do their work of putting away anyone who takes what belongs to us? Or is our aim something that sounds more righteous, namely, to be able to live an upright life in this world, without committing any crimes, in the hope that we will never have to pay a fine or serve time in prison?

Even in asking these questions, I'm afraid we expose a mindset far removed from the one God revealed to Job. Job was righteous, but look what happened to him. Within the confines of the popular attitude I just described, how can anyone respond adequately to Job or to the person who has been imprisoned by mistake? What can we say to the person who suffers greater harm in prison than he or she caused on the outside? How can we justify a system that spends more money to house the criminal than to pay back the victim?

If our answer is that these inadequacies and failures are too bad, but they only prove human fallibility, and that's why we need to work for prison reform, then we have not begun to think biblically. All of that may be true, but it says far too little. Ultimately, crime and punishment are about justice and injustice. And the cries from victims, as well as from unjustly treated offenders, are cries for justice. We offer little if any comfort to them by explaining that the system sometimes works. It will not soothe their aching hearts to learn that they aren't the first to have suffered unjustly.

No, the deeper answer we all long for when we cry for justice is the one Job was looking for when he asked, Why is there evil in the world? Who is responsible? Why try to live a righteous life or promote justice if injustice will occur anyway? If there is no hope of ultimate reconciliation, then why not give up? Why not become a cynic?

To treat these questions and judgments lightly would be to hide from reality. To limit ourselves as Christians to a narrow range of questions about prisons, police, and due process while ignoring all the unanswered questions about injustice is to close our minds to the wider context of our responsibility for promoting a just society under the sovereign lordship of Jesus Christ. Or if we tell people, whether inside or outside prisons, that they should put their trust in God for a future life and not worry about the injustices in this one, we force them and ourselves into a ridiculous corner. After all, why should anyone trust God to establish justice in the next life when he can't seem to run this world justly?

The question of justice, you see, is of one piece. It's about the character of God and his world. If we can't trust him to overcome the injustice of this world, why should we put any faith in his ability to pull it off the second time around?

A Wider and Deeper Justice

At this juncture, allow me to turn your attention to the second great Job in history: Jesus. Remember what he cried on the cross? "My God, my God, why have you forsaken me?" (Mark 15:34).

If Job was not righteous enough to keep from getting caught in God's war with Satan, then surely Jesus might have qualified for escape. How, then, could God have been so unjust as to turn over his only Son, a man perfect in all his ways, to the devil? If we consider Job's suffering a mystery, then surely we have to admit that the suffering of the Son of Man constitutes a far greater mystery.

You see, here again the larger questions of justice have to do with God's cosmic purposes in creating, restoring, and fulfilling his creation for his own glory. Yes, there are many detailed, smaller points of great importance within the larger drama. Yes, God himself gave Israel and his church many details of responsibility to fulfill with regard to the practice of justice and love. All those details are important. Properly appointed judges and officials *should* seek to uphold patterns of just retribution and distribution in public life. But ultimately, even the best constructed legal and political systems cannot answer the questions of why some people suffer and others do not, why some criminals get caught and others do not. Ultimately, like Job, we must cover our mouths before God when considering that innocent people sometimes suffer punishment and that human beings can do nothing whatever to restore life to those who become victims of murder.

We have no hope for true shalom, no answer to the cry for justice, within ourselves or solely from within our systems of justice. Ultimately our cry for justice must be directed to God, and the answers we wait for must come in God's good time, not according to the schedules we set. The God who could turn Job over to Satan, who could turn his own Son over to the people who nailed him to a cross, is a God with a wider and deeper conception of justice than we now have.

And here is where the good news of the gospel begins to penetrate our fog and darkness. The God who seemingly gives Job over to ruin and abandons his own Son is the God whose concern for justice turns out to be far greater than ours, extending far beyond the narrow details of distribution and retribution as we conceive them.

In a way we cannot yet understand, God's justice was sealed on the cross. There, Jesus bore the penalty for our sins so that God's perfect righteousness could be confirmed and established forever, never to be challenged again by any demon or human. And the God who seemed to act unjustly is the one who finally lifted his Son from death to make him the perfect Judge and King over all creation. The God who allowed Job to be reduced to nothing is the one who gave him sufficient hope, even in his deepest misery, to sing,

> I know that my Redeemer lives,
>   and that in the end he will stand upon the earth.
> And after my skin has been destroyed,
>   yet in my flesh I will see God;
> I myself will see him
>   with my own eyes—I, and not another .
>
> (19:25–27)

And at the end of his life, God restored Job to unanticipated glory and strength.

Working for Justice Now

But before you draw the conclusion that I have given up on this world and am now simply falling back on a wish for "pie in the sky by and by," let me take you back to the truth of the gospel as it bears on our present world. If victims of crime, along with a great many prisoners, cry for justice, our response to them must *not* be to say that there is no hope for justice in this world, but that their cries will be answered only in a future world after the Lord's return.

Rather, our response must be to demonstrate that, since God took on human flesh and suffered death in order to overcome evil in this world, we will choose to live by giving every ounce of our energy to promote justice. We will choose to encourage people to live just lives, to minister to those suffering injustice, to weep with those who weep, to urge sinners of all kinds to repent, *and* to seek reconciliation between victims and offenders.

Such a life is possible, of course, only in full dependence on God's justice in Christ, and that means living always in anticipation of the fullness of his shalom that is not yet complete. But the only way anyone—including you and I—can truly communicate that God is able to establish shalom in the future is by showing evidence of how God is dealing with injustice here and now.

We confess that God has overcome evil fundamentally in Jesus Christ, through the death and resurrection of his own Son. But the Son of God did not commission and send out his disciples to show people how to give up on this world, or to quit crying for justice, or to wait on the sidelines for Jesus' return in glory. That is not hope. It is a copout—a lie. To the contrary, Jesus told his disciples to take up the cross, to give up all illusions of their own righteousness, to realize that they would have to suffer, and to follow him in obedience to death. All along the way, the proof of their faithfulness to—and hope in—the justice of God in Christ would be demonstrated by the way they gave themselves to those around them—by preaching and demonstrating love and reconciliation now.

It is precisely through the hope of shalom in Christ's kingdom that God enables us to open our ears to the cry for justice coming from those around us. This is what allows us to identify with those who cry out and to endure to the end as we seek to overcome every form of injustice around us.

To live like this takes us directly into, and also beyond, issues of criminal justice. We must not limit ourselves to prison ministry or to seeking changes in the penal system. We must also work for a just education policy, for just health care policies, for economic justice, for environmental justice. Why? So that, if we work hard enough, we might be able to establish God's kingdom on earth by ourselves so we won't need to wait any longer for his shalom? Of course not. We work for justice now as a way for God to display tangible evidence—fruit-bearing results—of his open ear to the cry for justice.

God's mysterious work in Jesus Christ deals with injustice here and now on the way toward the full revelation of perfect shalom. In Christ, God is right now gathering up the fruits of his Spirit's work—fruits produced in the flesh by Jesus' brothers and sisters.

This very day, God is pointing through deeds of justice and reconciliation to his kingdom of shalom.

Righteous Public Servants

Do you know what it was that Job looked back on nostalgically
when he was suffering so much pain? He was not thinking primarily about his former health, wealth, good food, fine clothing.
No, Job looked back on the time when his greatest glory and pleasure came in the practice of justice—the justice that he knew
would one day be restored by his Redeemer:

> How I long for the months gone by,
>   for the days when God watched over me,
> when his lamp shone upon my head
>   and by his light I walked through darkness! . . .
> when I went to the gate of the city
>   and took my seat in the public square,
> The young men saw me and stepped aside
>   and the old men rose to their feet. . . .
> Whoever heard me spoke well of me,
>   and those who saw me commended me,
> because I rescued the poor who cried for help,
>   and the fatherless who had none to assist him.
> The man who was dying blessed me;
>   I made the widow's heart sing.
> I put on righteousness as my clothing;
>   justice was my robe and my turban.
> I was eyes to the blind
>   and feet to the lame.
> I was a father to the needy;
>   I took up the case of the stranger.
> I broke the fangs of the wicked
>   and snatched the victims from their teeth. . . .
> Men listened to me expectantly,
>   waiting in silence for my counsel.
> After I had spoken, they spoke no more;
>   my words fell gently on their ears. . . .
> I chose the way for them and sat as their chief;
>   I dwelt as a king among his troops;
>   I was like one who comforts mourners.
>   (29:2–25)

Let us freely cry out to God on behalf of all those who suffer injustice, pleading with him to make us righteous public servants like Job. Let us pray for renewed dedication to give our earthly lives for others, working diligently for justice with deep and sincere hope in the God who is reconciling all things to himself and who is already responding to our cry for justice in the shalom of Jesus Christ. Let us allow God to use us as evidence—as demonstration projects—of his justice so that people can begin to enjoy genuine hope in the fullness of his coming shalom. May we do everything "without grumbling or questioning," that we may be "blameless and innocent" (Phil. 2:14-15 RSV). Let us focus our attention and energy on what is true, honorable, and *just* (Phil. 4:8 RSV) so that we might serve as God's reconciling ministers, bearing testimony in our flesh to his complete reconciliation of all things:

> Therefore, if anyone is in Christ, he is a new creation; the old has gone, the new has come! All this is from God, who reconciled us to himself through Christ and *gave us the ministry of reconciliation:* that God was reconciling the world to himself in Christ, not counting men's sins against them. And he has committed to us the message of reconciliation. We are therefore Christ's ambassadors, *as though God were making his appeal through us.* We implore you on Christ's behalf: Be reconciled to God. God made him who had no sin to be sin for us, so that in him we might become the righteousness of God.
>
> (2 Cor. 5:17–21, emphasis added)

8

Free at Last

Don Holt

In this chapter, former prisoner Don Holt describes how the grace of God released him from a life of crime and punishment. Though this chapter is relatively short, it has an important place in this book and in this section on justice.

The odds of Don Holt's being a fifty-year-old freshman at Wheaton College and a student in the Colson Scholarship Program are astronomical, considering his background. He began to abuse drugs at age sixteen and soon moved on to theft and then to armed robbery. For twenty-five years he was in and out of prison.

This chapter describes Don's dramatic attempt to escape from McAlester prison in Oklahoma. He tells how God's grace saved him from being killed and then, in the quiet of solitary confinement, began filling his heart with godly sorrow. For the first time, he saw his victims as real people. And his heart was prepared to change when a stranger from the outside saw him as a real person, too, and reached out to share the gospel.

Don Holt's testimony is an example of what prison ministry is all about: a person living in crime and brutality who really becomes a new creature in Christ.

I came from a good family, yet I started using drugs at age fifteen. By the time I was sixteen, I was shooting heroin with a syringe.

I tried to renounce drugs when I was seventeen. At that age I had a religious or spiritual experience. Walking up to the altar at a Baptist church, something happened to me inside. I couldn't explain it. I got baptized, but there was no discipleship or nurturing of my infant faith. Within two weeks I was taking illegal drugs again.

For the next twenty to twenty-five years, my life was a shambles. Serious sin became habitual—taking drugs, learning how to be a bungling thief. I say "bungling" because I spent fourteen and a half calendar years in the Oklahoma State Prison, most of it in maximum security. I once spent fifteen months in the isolation unit. You may know it as solitary confinement. Yet each time I would go to prison, I would vow that it would be my last time.

I remember praying, in solitary, and asking God to help me. Good things would happen; someone would look on me with favor. People would say I was "lucky." I would get out of solitary confinement and eventually out of prison. Then I would go my own way, never thanking God or so much as giving him any thought. I would get a job. I would have things under my own control. I would do things my way.

For twenty-five years that was the pattern of my life—in and out of prison constantly. The second to last time I came out of prison, I vowed that I was smart enough to make it and avoid crime. I didn't even try, however. I got out and robbed stores immediately. I got away, too. As far as I was concerned, there was no God. I was stealing a lot of money; I didn't need God.

The Beginning of Change

I was eventually captured in Tulsa, Oklahoma, tried before a jury, and sentenced to five hundred years in the Oklahoma State Prison. When I went to prison that time, the only thing that I could think of doing was what every red-blooded American convict would do—escape.

I did escape! I went over the wall of McAlester Prison with two other men in 1976. It was the Saturday night before Easter. We drove a truck near the fence, climbed the scaffolding, and vaulted over. A guard was watching us, but our escape was such a shock to him that he didn't realize what was happening until two of us were over. Then pandemonium broke out. Sirens wailed. I recall thinking, "I'm going to get shot at any moment." When I went over the top of the fence, I got caught in the barbed wire. When I finally got out and hit the ground, I broke my leg at the ankle.

I was up and running as the first shot was fired. Somehow, even with a broken leg, I managed to stay out of the line of fire and get away. But I was recaptured the next day and put back in isolation. I heard from other guards that the tower guard had his clip out of his rifle when our escape attempt began. In his panic, as he attempted to put the clip in, the shells spilled all over the tower floor. That is why he could only shoot one time.

Later, I realized that God had spared my life. But he had allowed my leg to break so that I wouldn't get away. Why? Well, I didn't know what I was going to do after my escape. I just wanted to get away. I didn't have any solutions to my problems or to my miserable condition. I was a failure at everything. But God had a change in store for me.

In 2 Corinthians 7:10, Paul describes two kinds of sorrow—the sorrow of the world and godly sorrow. Well, at that point I had no idea what godly sorrow was. I was not sorry I escaped or committed a crime, I was just sorry I got caught! That had always been my attitude before, too. But this time, as I sat in isolation, I became aware that something had changed in my attitude and in my heart.

Before, I had looked at my incarceration as a kind of war with the state. If anybody got caught in it—like robbery victims—they were just casualties of the greater war. I did not care about victims, plain and simple. But now thoughts of the people I had hurt kept running through my head.

I kept remembering a moment when I was robbing a store. I had made everybody lie down on the floor. A white-haired woman was coming up the sidewalk, and I said to myself, "I hope she don't come in here." I hid behind a revolving bookcase. I had on my ski mask and a jumpsuit. She did come in. I jumped up behind her and yelled, "Get down on the floor; get behind that counter!"

She started crying. She got on the floor. Everything had worked out just fine for me. I had grabbed the money and fled. But now, back in solitary confinement, that scene haunted me. That woman reminded me of my mother.

A Change of Heart

I began to realize that in my heart I was seeing my victims as real people. I had never done that before; I always blocked that out of my mind. Now thoughts of my victims just started rolling in on me. I thought about my life, and how I was never going to get out of prison. I was never going to get a chance to prove anything to anyone. My life was just going to be a wasted, miserable existence.

Prisoners like me tell ourselves that "A man is an island," that what we do is our own business and does not affect other people. Well, what we do *does* affect other people greatly—our families most of all. I was beginning to see that.

I wanted to make restitution to my family and to the people who cared about me. That was godly sorrow. It was the first time in my life I had felt it. I really felt guilty for the things that I had done. I felt guilty just breathing other people's air.

About that time, I received a memorandum stating: "Rev. I. M. Judd wants to talk to you on the telephone." The memo said regulations did not permit this, but I could write him; it gave his address.

Here I was in Oklahoma. I had just escaped from a maximum security prison. I was in solitary confinement. And I had gotten a call from a person who claimed to be a "messenger of God." I thought that if anyone needed a message from God, I did. So I wrote him. He wrote back.

Now, I would never have listened to that man if he had said, "You know, I've got these Scriptures; I won't have anything else to do with you, but I've got these Scriptures for you to hear." But this guy wanted to be my friend. He followed up his letter by coming and visiting me. He had never been to a prison before.

One day I found out the story. He had met my brother on an airplane trip to California, and my brother had told him about my situation. The minister realized God wanted him to visit me, and he followed up on that conviction. His interest changed my life.

I have been out of prison since 1983! The Scripture says, "Let him that stole steal no more: but rather let him labour, working with his hands" (Eph. 4:28 KJV). For the last eight years, I have been "working with my hands." God has been faithful to me. In 1989 I received a pardon from the state of Oklahoma for every crime I ever committed. I came to Wheaton College in 1990 as a fifty-year-old freshman on a Colson Scholarship.

God has required me to tell other people about him, what he can do in somebody's life like mine because he has done so much for me! A man can dig a well so deep that he can't climb out by himself. I did, but God's grace lifted me out of that well of sin and crime.

9

The Future of Corrections in America

J. Michael Quinlan

As director of the United States Bureau of Prisons, J. Michael Quinlan is the "keeper" of more than 62,500 prisoners in America. We learn about the concept of justice from a man whose career has been spent working with the U.S. Justice Department.

He begins with an exposition of the statistics of prison overcrowding and then shares his vision for the future, a vision coming from a man who has the power and influence to make a difference. In sharing his goal of helping make prisoners whole again, he talks about the need for continuing education in the prisons and the availability of substance abuse programs.

He has already shown an example of helping prisoners toward wholeness by supporting the concept of community correctional centers. These are important in that they keep the prisoners near their families, their community, their church, and the community that can help with employment. Correctional centers are already in place in major cities such as New York, Chicago, Phoenix, and Los Angeles.

Mr. Quinlan has also used innovative programs such as homebound detention and electronic monitoring to lessen actual prison time. He has been supportive of the urban camp setting for nonviolent offenders.

A key to Mr. Quinlan's concept of practicing justice is to facilitate links to the community. He feels that the public has an obvious prejudice against offenders and needs to be educated. He also believes that the public has unrealistic expectations of what the prison system can realistically do. He believes that true rehabilitation depends on three factors: the correctional facility's effort, the individual inmate's choice, and the community's involvement. He concludes his chapter with a set of specific suggestions to strengthen the role of the volunteer as role model. He believes that volunteerism, especially in the religious sector, will make the greatest impact on the lives of prisoners.

In my relatively short tenure as the director of the Bureau of Prisons (four years now), I have come to the conclusion that without the help of volunteers, the prison services' ability to make a meaningful difference in offenders' lives is greatly limited.

To explain what I mean, let me start out by giving you a little bit of the backdrop about what is happening in the world of federal corrections, and share with you some of the things we are trying to do in an era when corrections is under increasing pressure to meet the challenges of growth and of society's expectations.

Our prison system at the federal level has grown dramatically. In 1981, we had 24,000 people in federal prisons. Now, just ten years later, we have 62,500 people. By the year 1995, 100,000 human beings are expected to be housed in federal institutions. That does not count the 710,000 men and women who are serving sentences in state institutions or those 350,000 people doing time in detention facilities. In 1991, in the United States, more than 1 million people lived in prison.

Most of our prisoners are serving sentences for drug offenses, a trend which has risen over the last ten years. In 1981, only 25 percent of federal prisoners were serving terms for drugs. In 1991, 55 percent of our 62,500 prisoners are serving terms for drugs. We expect that by 1995, 70 percent of an estimated one hundred thousand inmates will be serving terms for drugs.

The sentences of those who are serving terms for drugs are also increasing radically. In 1987, the average drug offender served a sentence of about twenty-seven months. In 1991, the average time served by a drug offender was seventy-eight months. This increase is partly due to the fact that parole is no longer available in the federal system—a result of a 1984 change in the law that went into effect in 1987. The new law created a system of guidelines that abolished the parole system for new offenders.

The longer sentences are also a result of the fact that Congress has enacted many laws that mandate minimum sentences. For drug-related crimes, these mandatory sentences are very severe. It is not uncommon to receive a fifteen- or twenty-year mandatory minimum sentence on a first or second conviction for certain drug offenses. Even the offense of carrying drugs, being a so-called "mule," carries a penalty of about ten years.

This trend obviously concerns correctional administrators, who are having to manage institutions that are more and more crowded. The space we need to house prisoners is simply not becoming available at the same rate that new offenders are coming in. Despite the fact that we have a number of new prisons under construction in the federal system, we still operate at 161 percent of our capacity. This means that we have about 39,000 cells and rooms for 62,500 prisoners, and most of these are double-bunked.

Strategies for Hope

The reality of more prisoners with longer sentences means that more and more people have less hope for their future. Their community attachments are threatened by the fact that they are going to be away from their families and their communities for such a long time. We in the Bureau of Prisons are acutely aware of this concern, particularly because we see and hear from prisoners about their desperate need for some light at the end of the tunnel.

To help alleviate this hopelessness, we have been trying to put together programs within our institutions that meet not only the prisoners' educational and work needs, but also their spiritual and other needs. For instance, we are putting into place what we consider to be state-of-the-art drug treatment programs for the approximately 47 percent of the population who have moderate to serious substance abuse histories.

The Bureau of Prisons is fortunate in not having a lot of drug or alcohol abuse within the walls of its institutions. We conduct frequent urinalysis tests to deter it. For those who want help, we offer what we consider to be excellent substance-abuse treatment. This is followed up by community-based substance-abuse treatment during the first six months after release, when relapses are especially likely to occur.

We also have launched a number of initiatives to improve the literacy level of our prisoners. In 1982, we mandated for the first time that prisoners would have to achieve a sixth-grade reading level. We found that so successful that in 1986 we raised the required reading level to eighth grade. Inmates who fail to achieve that goal are not eligible for the best jobs or preferred quarters or similar privileges. As of 1991, we are proud to say we have raised the mandatory requirement to achievement of a GED (high school equivalency diploma). I believe this requirement will have a significant impact on our prisoners' ability to compete for jobs and other opportunities in the community when they are released. (And all but a few of them will eventually be released.)

Some people argue that we should not give prisoners opportunities that are not readily available to the average citizen. Why, they ask, should we provide prisoners with state-of-the-art drug treatment when there is a sixth-month waiting list in the community for such programs? Why should we give prisoners vocational or educational opportunities when free citizens cannot afford those programs? Obviously, we in corrections feel that the benefits of these programs—for society as well as for offenders—make them worthwhile. But we must walk a very careful line to be sure that we don't make our programs so attractive that the public thinks they are "too good" for prisoners.

Community-Based Alternatives

We in the Bureau of Prisons believe in a "continuum of sanctions," with restrictions that vary with the severity of crime and the threat to the community. In addition to our institutional programs, therefore, we are exploring several forms of community sanctions to replace incarceration for some offenders.

Community sanctions have typically taken the form of halfway houses or similar facilities under contract for the Bureau of Prisons and operated by the Salvation Army, the Volunteers of America, or other community service groups. In the traditional halfway house model, prisoners live at the center but work in the community, find recreation in the community, and visit family in the community. But such halfway houses, in my view, are only one example of the kinds of intermediate punishment we should be offering across the nation for federal offenders.

One alternative model we have been exploring is the "day prison" concept. In this model, prisoners live at home but report daily to community corrections centers for work and treatment. We also are embarked on a number of pilot projects to explore the possibilities of home detention (with or without electronic monitoring) and urban work camp programs, which allow prisoners to live in community facilities but work at a federal military base or other government institution. We believe if we can convince judges and the public that such centers are tough enough, that they provide sufficient punishment, the courts will utilize such alternative sanctions more readily.

The Bureau of Prisons is very interested in the opportunities in the community that we provide to offenders, but you must realize that we are not in total control over which inmates participate in such programs. You might say why, if you have 62,500 prisoners and you are interested in community sanctions, aren't you putting more of those people in community facilities?

As you might suspect, the answer is complex. Placing some inmates in community facilities requires the concurrence of the judge. It also needs to fit within a logical description, determined by the United States Sentencing Commission, of who can go to the community.

The Sentencing Commission was created by Congress in 1984, and part of its purpose is to stipulate which inmates can serve their sentences in a community-based facility.

The Department of Justice is currently working with the Sentencing Commission to optimize the number of categories of offenders who can serve their sentences in a community facility. But this is an uphill struggle in a country that doesn't feel safe on its streets, that feels threatened, victimized, and suffocated by criminal activity. Negotiating with Congress and the Sentencing Commission to achieve appropriate flexibility in putting people in the community is proving to be quite a challenge—but we are continuing our efforts.

Building Bridges of Understanding

In the past, I believe that federal correctional administrators like myself and my counterparts in the fifty states have done a relatively poor job of educating the public as to what prisons are all about, what initiatives we have embarked upon, and what kinds of help we really need. Over the past four or five years, however, we in the Bureau of Prisons have embarked on a conscientious effort to bring the public into our institutions. One of the major ways we have done this is through the establishment of Community Relations Boards at most of our institutions. These boards are made up of concerned individuals from the community, both elected and nonelected, who meet with the top staff of institutions on a regular basis, generally every month or every other month, to talk about issues of concern either to the community or to the institution. Time and time again, we have found that bringing the people into our institutions decreases the mystique of the correctional facility and helps establish realistic expectations as to what policies and programs should be implemented.

My strong belief is if we can make more and more people aware of what we are doing, and how we are doing it, we can make a positive change in how our future tax dollars will be spent. This is a crucial point of education for all of us. Regardless of what we feel about crime and our current system of justice, if we continue the trend of locking more and more people up for longer periods of time, we are all going to have to give more and more of our tax dollars to corrections. The correctional path we have chosen as a nation is a very costly one.

Just in the Bureau of Prisons, which operates sixty-eight institutions and represents about 7 percent of the Americans who are in correctional facilities, our budget has more than doubled in the past four years. Forecasts say that it will probably double again in the next four years. Locking people up is a very expensive way to deal with the crime problem. For financial reasons alone, I am convinced prisons must be a scarce corrections resource, reserved for those who require a secure environment. Those who do not should be punished with other forms of sanctions.

The Rehabilitation Equation

I have been with the Bureau of Prisons for twenty years now. I am very proud of my association with this agency, which was founded in 1930 and has had only five people as its director. I am humbled when I look at some of the people who have held my position in the past. But I feel I have been given a wonderful opportunity and I have tried to use it to respond in a more proactive manner to some of the issues. In the process, I have learned a tremendous amount from people around the world who are dealing with similar issues—often times in very different ways.

One of the things that struck me recently is that the media and the public tend to hold corrections to a much higher standard than we could ever live up to. The public's general expectation is that people who go to prison should be rehabilitated. After all, they reason, we have these individuals as captive audiences during the time they are in prison; why shouldn't we "cure" them? Of course, we are dealing with a very difficult group of people to start with. Most have had difficult personal histories ranging from poverty to unspeakable abuse. Many never learned concepts like right, wrong, and delayed gratification. And many are long-term substance abusers as well. Yet the public doesn't really fully understand these problems. They challenge us when we tell them that half the people we release from prison will be back in prison in three years. They look at us in an accusing way and say, "You have failed to deliver the services and the kinds of training you should have while that person was with you."

I used to listen to those accusations and feel guilty. I felt that they were right, that I had failed. Because some of these prisoners went out and committed new crimes, I assumed that in some way the institutions to which these prisoners were assigned had not done everything they could have.

Then I realized that there is more to rehabilitation than what the correctional facility delivers. Rehabilitation is, in my view, a three-part responsibility, an equation that adds up only when all three elements are present.

It is true that the correctional facility has the responsibility to provide adequate resources for rehabilitation—education opportunities, literacy and job skills training, substance abuse treatment, and so on. Through positive inmate relationships with staff, we can try to promote what we believe are mainstream social values. But we cannot do it all. The rehabilitation equation has two other elements as well.

The second crucial element in rehabilitation is the individual prisoner's free choice. We have not yet found a magic elixir to change people's attitudes. It is hard to get into the heart and soul of another human being, and we just haven't found a sure way to do it. We may do all the right things in offering programs and opportunities for prisoners. Ultimately, however, the decision to change and to remain crime free must rest deep within a person's heart.

The third critical element in our equation is positive community attitude and involvement. In most communities of the United States, someone who has been convicted and sent to prison is considered a total outcast from society. And that, I think, is the heart of what is wrong with American corrections. I think until we are able to somehow get the community to take a degree of ownership for an offender while he or she is in prison, we will never ever change his or her behavior. We will never improve our recidivism rates. We will never be the success that we want to be in helping incarcerated human beings successfully re-enter society.

I believe the time has come—not just here in the United States but in other countries as well—for a national initiative. We need to bring the community into the process of helping correctional administrators rehabilitate felons. And this can be done, I believe, through volunteer programs. If we can encourage more people to come into our institutions to tutor those who cannot read or write, to counsel those who have substance abuse or emotional problems, to model mainstream values, to befriend those who have very few supportive relationships, I believe we can make a difference for many human beings.

Even more important than such community involvement in the prisons is community involvement with prisoners who have been released, particularly during the first six to nine months after prisoners are released. That is the time when relapses generally occur, when decisions are made to return to criminal behavior because job opportunities or meaningful relationships are just not there. If every inmate had a volunteer friend to counsel, to be supportive, I think we could make a significant dent in our recidivism rates.

Now, some might say that such follow-up is the responsibility of the probation service—that professionals have the resources and the training to guide the newly released offender. Certainly the probations staff plays an important role in monitoring the behavior of offenders in the community. But that is not the helping, supportive role that in many cases the prisoner needs. A professional is simply not the same as a friend.

How to encourage others to become involved in such a volunteer initiative is the challenge I face. I have been working to develop a relationship with a national organization that would work with federal offenders in our sixty-eight institutions and give us the network that we need to make this volunteer program a reality. And we currently have about 2,800 people who volunteer their services in either religious, counseling, or tutoring programs in federal institutions. But we have 62,500 men and women in these prisons. That means we need 62,500 volunteers, not to mention those we would need for offenders in our community-based facilities.

You may say that's impossible—"You're not going to do it." I am an eternal optimist, however. I believe in the spirit of faith. And I believe we can make a difference if we promote change and put the needed resources behind it. I am committed to trying to make a difference. It is a vital mission.

10

Is the Justice System Just?

Gordon McLean

Justice and the abuse of civil rights are incompatible. In this chapter, Gordon McLean, who has worked as a helping professional with gangs both in Chicago and San Jose, California, speaks of the violations of juvenile rights both at the hands of police and in the courts. To a young person on the street, McLean says, a finding of "guilty" is not justice, but a word a young black man hears from a white person in judicial robes.

McLean has been a court observer and testifying witness for many years. He speaks with authority when he says the courts are not capable of dealing with the full spectrum of issues involved in juvenile crimes. To do justice within the chaotic inner city life of the juvenile, he says, we must look at the broader issues of dysfunctional homes, poor schools, and the lack of jobs.

McLean characterizes the inner city as a battleground where he has attended far more funerals than weddings. As he seeks justice for young people, he is particularly upset by politicians who, he believes, should know better when they advocate the quick fix of imprisonment, rather than long-term solutions for the juvenile criminals who live in urban settings.

Earlier this year, police officers beat a suspect while twenty-one of their colleagues watched. The nation was aroused, thanks to an alarming videotape taken by an amateur observer. A few days later, five New York City police officers were charged in the death of a burglary suspect they confronted. Washington, Atlanta, and Denver reported other incidents of violence.

What was amazing to those of us familiar with the problems of the urban streets of America's large cities was that these incidents surprised anyone! Each was tragic, and one was videotaped, but the problem is not new. There is more law at the end of a police officer's nightstick than in the Supreme Court, and cops seem determined to keep it that way.

In Chicago, the police superintendent boasts that his department is "the biggest gang in the city," and many of us in Chicago agree. In this city last year, slightly more than 2 percent of the police brutality complaints were upheld. This track record shows what a futile route it is to complain to the Police Office of Professional Standards.

Last year the Los Angeles police department paid out more than eight million dollars in damages to victims of excessive force.

In Chicago, police arrest young people for wearing colored jackets, sweaters, and shoelaces, although what may be gang colors on one street are school colors a few blocks away. Kids are arrested for disorderly conduct and mob action and either taken to the station or dropped off in a rival gang's territory. Their offense may be nothing worse than coming home from the store or school with some of their friends.

In serious cases, police often dispense with little technicalities such as the suspect's right to remain silent and have an attorney present for questioning. If they want a confession, they will get it, by fair means or foul. In Illinois, a police youth officer is supposed to be present to see that a minor is not abused by other officers. But that young person really needs an attorney!

A Kid's View of Justice

The court system increasingly seeks to try serious juvenile offenders as adults without any concern as to whether the adult system is capable of meeting the needs of kids. It isn't. And Illinois, among all the states that mandate the transfer of juveniles to adult court, allows for no review of that decision by either juvenile or adult court.

The kids on the street have even learned a new way to get even with a rival. They simply name him as the shooter in an attempted murder or homicide. The police are happy to cooperate because a quick identification clears a case. Whether the suspect so named actually committed the crime seems of little concern.

"Guilty" to you and me is a statement of moral condemnation, something of which to be ashamed. To a street kid, it's what a white man in a black robe downtown says when your luck runs out.

The juvenile court remains a remarkably effective means of dealing with young offenders, mostly because of the dedication of the probation officers. But these men and women have few resources to help them in their task, and the challenges they face are formidable. Homes are broken and dysfunctional. Schools turn the other way as kids drop out or are pushed out on the streets. The federal government's priority is to support cities overseas and ignore the broken core of America's urban blight. Jobs are few and far between; the neighborhood drug dealer is often the quickest and most generous employer of kids.

The problems of inner-city youth will not be solved easily. With violence on the rise and the weaponry of the streets getting more sophisticated, an urban youngster's chances of just growing up are getting slimmer. And sometimes those who work with these kids just have to feel that few people outside the battleground of the inner city are very concerned.

"During every one hundred hours on our streets, we lose three times more young men than were killed in one hundred hours of ground war in the Persian Gulf. Where are the yellow ribbons of hope and remembrance. . . . Where is the concern, the heartfelt commitment to support the children of this war?" pointedly asks Health and Human Services Secretary Louis Sullivan.

Working with young people, which has been my life calling, I expect to spend time performing weddings and I have seen some beautiful ones. But I've been to far more funerals for young victims of the street. I've spent too many hours at hospital emergency rooms with a family, praying that a son or daughter might survive the bullet wounds threatening his or her life. I've had too many mothers, sisters, and girlfriends crying in my arms as the life of a loved one ebbed away.

Then I've seen other tragedies in courtrooms where young people were tried as adults to satisfy the cry of the public outrage for vengeance. I've watched as kids caught up in the violence of their crazy world—and with every potential to turn their lives into something good—were sent to prison for most of the rest of their lives. I've listened to families cry over tragedies that should not be.

A Voice of Sanity

I expect the secular world to be confused, angry, bitter, wanting nothing but punishment. I expect the cynics and the hateful to insist that more prison cells be built, that young offenders be tried as adults, and sentences lengthened. There is no surprise in what they demand.

But I find it sad to see this same hollow, hopeless reasoning coming from our church people—people whose whole life commitment to the Christian gospel is to believe that people can change. We need to hear the Christian community talking of biblical restitution and reconciliation, of Christian conversion, of the God of a second chance and a new beginning.

We also need to minister to the victims who sadly and often vainly look for relief from their hurt in what a judge does in a courtroom. How temporary and fragile that action becomes. The fact is, the hurt of a serious crime victim is far too deep and lasting for any court action to relieve. The care and compassion and healing our Lord offers through his people is the answer these victims need and so infrequently find. Modern day Good Samaritans can bring the touch of Jesus to broken and hurting victims.

Certainly the company of the committed needs to be a voice for sanity and reason in a justice system gone awry. In not too many years, if we keep up the present trends, half our American population will be in jail and the other half will be prison guards! That is a cost in human life and dollars we can no longer afford. We need to look at alternatives—home monitoring, intensive probation, community service, education, and job training—to help redirect the broken lives of offenders who want to change. As judges, police, lawyers, probation officers, counselors, jurors, correctional staff, or concerned citizens—however, wherever our life path intersects the road of crime, drug abuse, and despair—we need to be offering new life and new hope.

Things will not change much as long as legislators see the road to re-election paved with competition to be the most "tough on crime." No one wants to be soft on crime. But let's start being realistic and turn the system around, not just blindly strike out. What counts is not how many offenders we lock up, but how many can be turned into good citizens.

The gospel of Jesus Christ can do that. That fact can no longer be the best kept secret in the whole justice system. We Christians need to be on the front lines of our criminal justice system, taking that message and offering it to the hurting, disillusioned kids on our streets and in our cell blocks. The future of our nation may hinge on how we respond.

Part 5

The Future
of Prison Ministry

Introduction

Prison ministry has a bright future. I believe more and more churches are coming to realize that prisons and jails—more than four thousand in the United States—represent one of the great unharvested mission fields. More and more Christians are volunteering to help with the harvest.

Who Is a Prison Ministry Volunteer?

Sixty thousand volunteers are presently involved in prison ministry. These men and women represent a diverse cross-section of ages, occupations, and denominations. Yet despite their diversity, the volunteers I meet share four important qualities: perseverance, caring, patience, and determination.

Determination is certainly needed to work in a ministry that runs counter to public opinion in many areas. As we have seen, the general public is concerned, fearful, and angry when it comes to crime. Compassion for offenders is not likely to be a popular stance.

Prison ministry volunteers, too, are concerned about our soaring crime rate. But unlike politicians who rely on rhetoric such as "Let's get tough on crime" and "Let's put these criminals away," prison ministry volunteers realize that crime is symptomatic of spiritual drought. Only prison ministry, therefore, addresses the root causes of crime. When a man or woman gets right with God and turns away from sin, then we see true regeneration. And only such regeneration can reduce the recidivism rate.

Prison ministry volunteers are acutely aware that criminals are not a special breed, a bad seed, as some would think. We are *all* sinners, all capable of committing crimes.

Not too long ago, a large convention was held in a Cape Cod hotel. Police were called in when drunken conventioneers committed numerous crimes. They pulled twenty-two fire alarms, sprayed fire extinguishers, broke the ice machines, and stole two television sets. "Hooligans!" someone might say. "Felons!" someone else might assert. "Sounds like juvenile delinquents on a rampage," another might remark. Unfortunately the convention was a gathering of the Massachusetts Police Association, and the inebriated criminals were all police officers. Even the defenders of the law have the same nature as any other person.

This deep understanding of human nature is what gives most volunteers in prison ministry their compassion and understanding. They begin by looking at themselves and acknowledging their own sinfulness. Then they find it easier to see the prisoner as a three-dimensional person.

The volunteers also realize that everyone has the same basic needs, to be loved, to feel support, to have friendship, to receive respect, and to feel self-esteem. Prison ministry volunteers know well that without these essential components, which God has built into the human experience, anyone can become warped and thwarted in their development and growth.

Strengths and Weaknesses

How many prison ministries are there, where are they, and what are they doing?

Institute for Prison Ministries research has answered these questions. In a recent survey (March 1991), IPM catalogued 473 separate prison ministries and an additional 1,200 mom-and-pop organizations. Some of these ministries have been in existence for thirty or more years, others for ten years, and some for merely a month.

Overall, the strength of prison ministries in America lies in two areas: evangelism and discipleship. Our primary weakness is aftercare. We know that this is a problem because less than 20 percent of all released Christian inmates ever find a home church. To change these statistics, Christian halfway houses and transitional living facilities are needed, especially those connected directly to local churches. Newly released inmates need to be paired up with

Christian volunteers who will support them and help with basic survival skills.

Another overall weakness that affects everyone in prison ministry is the fact that ministries don't work together, even when it seems logical and natural.

Several years ago, while visiting a large city in Michigan, I convened all the people in that city who worked in prison ministry. I had a luncheon for them and then updated them on some of our research. Thirty people attended, representing the Salvation Army, the Full Gospel Businessmen's Association, and several local ministries. And I was surprised to learn that not only had they not worked together; in some cases, they did not even know each other. Several of the men at the meeting did not believe that women should be involved in jail and prison ministry, although several of the leaders present were women. Most used doctrine and theology, personal feelings and opinions, to accentuate differences rather than look for common ground and points of agreement.

Unfortunately, I have learned that such division is characteristic of prison ministries in many cities. And I have observed three principal reasons for ministries not working together:

(1) *Territorialism.* This is basically a way of saying "I was here first." People claim a specific institution or geographical area where they have developed a ministry and feel competition when others come along later.

(2) *Competition for money.* This is a real concern. A worsening economy means resources are limited. Ministries are acutely aware of having to compete for their share of the pie.

(3) *The need for attention.* This often translates into proving who is doing the *best job.* Sometimes inflating statistics are meant to prove that one ministry is more successful than another.

Why We Need Each Other

These are all understandable reasons—but they're not good enough. There are two compelling reasons why ministries should strive to overcome their differences and work together:

They represent the body of Christ.
They need each other.

The Scriptures tell us that each person and ministry has distinctive gifts and a specific role to play. Besides, the problems we are facing with crime and incarceration in America greatly overwhelm the number of ministries and volunteers presently working. Even sixty thousand volunteers (some of whom are inactive) are not enough to match a prison population that doubled in the last six years to more than a million. As crime continues to escalate, we also need volunteers to reach out to the one in four families who will be the victim of some type of crime.

Another reason for an increased need for the involvement of churches and volunteers now is based upon my belief that access to inmates will become more narrow in the future. For financial reasons, the number of prison visitations is being reduced by wardens in many states. This in turn limits the number of religious volunteers allowed in. We must keep in mind that access to prisoners is a policy and not a right. While prisoners have a right to religious access, the number of volunteers and the types of organizations can still be dictated by the warden.

I believe the future will call for more volunteer leaders—that is, volunteers who are equipped to screen other volunteers, recruit them, train them, and supervise them. With the impact of the current recession and with so many families living from paycheck to paycheck, we will not be able to afford the luxury of a ministry with a large paid staff to do these tasks. It will be essential that ministries provide for the training these volunteer leaders will need.

In many states, prison chaplains are being phased out in a formal way. In the summer of 1991, the state of Georgia, for example, eliminated all full-time paid chaplains. This trend toward eliminating chaplain positions underlines the need for training volunteers. In one state I recently met several volunteer chaplains, and I was shocked at how deficient they were in both formal education and biblical knowledge. I'm not suggesting that seminary and ordination is essential to being an effective chaplain, but some level of training and accountability is desirable.

In the federal system, often a model, there are chaplains who give regional supervision. The office of Charles Riggs, one of the authors of this book, has had the highest standards for his chaplains for over a decade. Sadly, this is not always the case in the state systems. There are two ways to remedy this for the future. If a state will not support chaplains, then I recommend that a coalition of local churches call and financially support a chaplain for their local institution. This is entirely consistent with biblical teaching and adds the essential ingredient of accountability.

To insure that inmates will be exposed to knowledgeable people, volunteers will have to increase their knowledge and understanding in areas of theology and biblical knowledge. Volunteers will also need to be trained in evangelistic principles and methodologies.

For some time, we have assumed that individuals in prison ministry who rise to levels of leadership have all the management skills necessary. We now know this is not true. The ability to communicate clearly, manage time effectively, and manage resources and people skillfully, is just as essential in ministry as it is in industry and business.

A Good Heart Is Not Enough

We may be seeing a dissolution of the estimated fifteen hundred mom-and-pop prison ministry organizations across America. These volunteers are often very sincere and warmhearted individuals who give of their personal resources, working out of their local church. They have no organization, usually no formal mission statement, no systematic way of raising funds, and no board that can assess their goals.

I remember being in the kitchen of a husband and wife who had their own prison ministry. They had several telephones on their kitchen wall. One phone represented a hot line for teenage runaways. Another was a crisis line for drug and alcohol abuse. The third doubled as their home phone and their prison ministry office phone. I thought it was commendable that these people wanted to help so many people, but in some areas they might have lacked the expertise to do a really good job.

For many years we have said that anyone with sincere compassion for prisoners should have equal access to prisoners. But we don't let just any good-hearted citizens, even the most caring, teach our children. We require our teachers to have a college degree and certification. And there are many sincere, compassionate people who have a message to give us in church, but we wouldn't want them to become the pastor of the church. Most pastors go to seminary, are examined by other clergy, and are then ordained and often endorsed by a denomination.

I believe we are moving into an era where there will be an important role for good-hearted, caring people in aftercare, where they can help inmates with transition issues like acquiring job skills, finding a temporary residence, and settling into a church. Those who spend the most time in prisons, however—especially as the numbers are reduced by the institutions themselves— ought to be professionals who meet minimum standards of training and certification and are accountable to an authority who can both observe and appraise their work.

I have believed for many years that one reason so many people start their own jail and prison ministry is a fear of accountability. Unfortunately, this has sometimes led to ineffective or even harmful practices. We need to remember that not everything done in the name of the Lord—or in the name of prison ministry—is good. There are already too many "lone rangers" in this area of ministry. To stay on track, we all need both the support and the loving review of our fellow Christians.

A fine example of two prison ministries working together is Prison Fellowship and the Bill Glass organization. Prison Fellowship has concentrated in discipleship for fifteen years, and Bill Glass has been involved in frontline evangelism for twenty years. In 1990, these two organizations found a logical way to work together.

Prison Fellowship volunteers in a local community now do the follow-up with prisoners who have made a commitment or a recommitment to Christ during a "Weekend of Champions," Bill Glass's evangelistic effort in prisons. Inmates notice when ministries work together like this. I believe our example is as important as our words.

The partnership of Bill Glass and Prison Fellowship is a good one for another reason. They have not tried to swallow up each other's identity. Each one is still distinct and autonomous. Each one does what God has gifted them to do best. But they are working together because they know they need each other.

So often ministries get caught up in the futile debate over who gets the credit. I believe we in prison ministry need a humble attitude and a willingness to compromise and cooperate. Ministries do that when they abide by the rules and policies of the institution. We should do the same when we work with one another.

For the future of prison ministry, I continue to see more networking. Ministries must ask themselves what they do best and what other type of work would complement theirs. Then they should seek to work with other prison ministries that provide the complementary skills.

Beyond a Numbers Mentality

I've been happy to see that over the last five years, for the most part, prison ministries have concentrated less on how many decisions were made and more on the quality of the decision, less on compiling statistics and more on developing relationships with inmates. I believe this emphasis is vital.

Statistics, after all, can be misleading. Here's an example. In 1990, 89,480 prisoners were released from prison and 9,870,546 were released from jails. How many of these are Christians? We can make a good estimate by considering how many decisions for Christ were made that year in prisons and jails. In 1990, Good News Jail and Prison Ministry reported 16,609 decisions for Christ. The Salvation Army reported 11,862 decisions. The Bill Glass organization reported 10,500 decisions. If we add in the approximately 100,000 decisions that come through chaplains in local jails, state facilities, and federal institutions, we can estimate that about 138,971 decisions for Christ were made in 1990.

From there, percentage-wise, we could estimate that about 10,000 Christians are released from prison each year. But if we truly had 10,000 Christians coming out of prison each year, we would see massive revival across America. And that isn't happening. Many of those decisions fall by the wayside. And one reason this happens is a hit-or-miss approach that neglects to disciple prisoners adequately after they make a decision and, especially, after they are released.

I do not believe you can lead someone to Christ in five minutes. Helping an inmate decide to follow God requires first developing a relationship with that inmate and helping him understand the authority of the Bible and the person and claim of Jesus Christ. It may require weeks, months, or years of loving overtures and prayers. It will require waiting for the Holy Spirit to do his work.

After that, of course, the decision *can* be made in five minutes—but someone must prepare the way. And the work isn't finished after the decision is made. Someone must stick around to help the new Christian grow.

With this in mind, we should not be discouraged if we have spent a year working with an inmate planting seeds and then that inmate makes a decision for Christ at someone else's weekend crusade. We have to be as content to plow the fields as we are to reap the harvest. And to do this, we must keep in mind our overall purposes. As Oswald Chambers once said, "We are not to make men converts of our opinions, we are to make them disciples of Christ."

When I was sharing the gospel with prisoners in the state of Connecticut recently, I was told that a certain inmate in lockdown was a Christian. As I began talking to this young inmate, I asked him if he had a Bible. He said he had many. So I asked him to look up 2 Corinthians 4. He flipped through some pages, but I noticed he was in Deuteronomy. I helped him find 2 Corinthians and asked him to read a portion of chapter 4. It soon became clear that this prisoner was both functionally illiterate and biblically illiterate.

Now, I am not saying that a person who can't read cannot be a Christian. I wouldn't presume to say that young man did not have a genuine encounter with the living Lord. And yet I think of him whenever I see decision statistics. It would have been easy to put that young man's name on a small card and make him a statistic. Working with him, praying with him, reading the Bible to him, teaching him to read for himself, helping him grow—that's an entirely different matter.

In order to make disciples out of inmates who make a decision for Christ, the prison ministry evangelist and discipler need to pass more information to each other. When I was a probation officer, I sought out and passed along much information about a client to pertinent parties such as the judge, the defense, the prosecution, the residential treatment center, or even the department of corrections. That information included

family history,
childhood experiences,
church experiences,
education,
job history,
health,
financial history,
self-image, and
experiences with failures.

Although the headings for the court reports were different, most of this information was worked in to an average twenty- or thirty-page report.

In prison ministry, however, we don't usually listen for or gather such crucial information or pass it on to other ministries who will do follow-up work. Someone could easily say, "Well, that takes too much work." And yet the secular system does such histories to convict people and to sentence them. Can we whose whole purpose is to love inmates to the Lord do less?

I've administered the Colson Scholarship Program at Wheaton College for more than four years. And I find that the key people who have said they worked with these offenders—the chaplain or the prison ministry worker—often don't pass on significant information. And this is usually because they have never asked the questions!

A Ministry of Reconciliation

When I think of prison ministry, I invariably think of Mother Consuella York. Now in her sixties, she is an angel who wears black garments—and a model for others to follow in this ministry. For more than forty years, she has brought the gospel to the more than 7,500 prisoners in Cook County Jail. And she has never missed a day. After slipping on ice and breaking her leg, she just ministered in a cast.

Mother York is short, yet her size should never fool anyone. I was recently with her in the jail gymnasium with five hundred inmates. A judge was speaking, and some of the inmates began to heckle. Mother York simply turned and pointed a stern index finger. And a hush fell over the audience. That is the kind of respect she commands!

In the 1950s, as the daughter of an African-American minister, she felt the call to ministry and ordination. Her father and the church elders told her clearly that a woman had no leadership role in the church. Still she listened to the call she heard from God. Eventually she became an ordained Baptist minister.

Jail ministry, too, was not a place for women in 1950. But Consuella York is a person who has never worried about public opinion. She just worried whether her life was consistent with the teachings of Jesus Christ. She continued to listen to God, and she followed him into the jail.

Perhaps nothing so exemplifies Mother York's ministry as what Dr. John Perkins refers to as the Christian's "call to reconciliation." In the early sixties, Mother York's husband was killed in the course of a robbery. Her husband's murderer was subsequently locked on her cellblock in the jail. The inmates incarcerated with the murderer approached Consuella York with a proposition: "We'll take care of him!" They meant, of course, they would kill him. Characteristic of her life and her commitment to Christ, she responded, "He doesn't need violence; he needs Jesus!"

She was willing to forgive even her husband's murderer and to protect the life of a man who had caused her so much personal pain and grief.

Anyone who has ever come in contact with Consuella York knows that she epitomizes prison ministry through dedication, tireless effort, efforts toward reconciliation, and a deep commitment to Christ.

She says of herself,

I'm just a little old lady from a Baptist background where women were not allowed to do anything but go to church and Sunday school. But one day I heard him loud and clear. God didn't ask for my femininity. God didn't ask for my culture. God didn't ask for my calling card. So even though I was poor and low and black, I had no choice but to hear him and follow.

And hear him she did. She said, as Isaiah had said, "Here I am, send me!" This good and gentle lady, with the presence of a lamb, goes into the lion house where the creatures are wild and wicked, and she tames them. She tames them not with a whip and chair, but with the Word of God. God's Word on her lips and in her hands is a flaming sword in an environment where the enemy has already claimed most prisoners.

We, too, must keep in mind the implications of spiritual warfare. The enemy clearly has a claim on people who have been overtly sinful. But Jesus has also made a claim on these same people. And as we venture into the jails and prisons, we are literally on the frontline of the war between God and the powers of darkness. That is why we need spiritual preparedness and the willingness to "tough it out" when we have challenges and setbacks.

A Message to Society

I am convinced that we who work in prisons have an important message to send to society—and a responsibility to send it. In our work, we have the chance to observe the end product of our nation's policies and attitudes toward crime and criminals. It is up to us to try to influence both the policies and change the attitudes.

I once had a long meeting with a state legislator. She totally agreed with me that overcrowding is reducing our prisons' ability to treat prisoners humanely. I recommended reducing the numbers of nonviolent offenders in prison and adding more community-based alternatives. I also asked for a more compassionate approach to punishment in America.

That legislator listened for more than ninety minutes and then said, "I totally agree with you, but I can't publicly recommend those things. Such a stand would be politically unpopular."

She was right, of course. When it comes to prisons, compassion *is* politically incorrect. But for the future we need to do more to get our message across. We need to influence lawmakers to listen to our concerns. And we need to elect politicians and legislators who have the courage of their convictions, who will listen to and act on commonsense arguments about the rehabilitation of offenders.

After all, one does not have to be a Christian to recognize that biblical concepts like restitution make good sense. One does not have to be a theologian to recognize that revenge and retaliation almost always create a more bitter and hardened criminal.

And one does not have to be a psychologist to understand that relationships, friendships, a support system, practical job skills, and education all increase the chances of a prisoner's success when he or she is released. The church must continue to make these commonsense recommendations to society at large.

We must be politically astute in doing so, of course. I once heard a prison ministry volunteer impart to a group of community citizens a guarantee of 100 percent success—no recidivism. That kind of statement is foolish. There is no quick fix, no easy solution, to the problem of crime in America. Even the alternatives will be costly. But I'm convinced they offer us our only hope for a positive solution to the problem of crime in America.

A Message to the Church

We in prison ministry also have a message to impart to the church, to our fellow members of the body of Christ. And that message concerns who we are and who Christ has called us to be. In essence, it's a message that criminals can change, people can repent and be forgiven. We in the church are called to be agents of that change by reaching out to prisoners in love and in obedience to God's call.

We won't reach everyone, of course. On two occasions I met Richard Speck, the criminal who coined the term "mass murder" by killing nine student nurses in Chicago in the early sixties. In prison, he consistently abused himself by inhaling paint thinner and a homemade alcohol that kept him constantly inebriated. I wasn't surprised to hear he had died in prison at age forty-nine. What is most shocking about Speck is that he never showed any remorse for his victims. There is no evidence that he regretted his crime or ever turned to God.

And yet God has clearly gifted human beings—even prisoners—with a conscience. A conscience prompts us to remorse, to contrition, to repentance. A conscience is one indication of an alive spirit. What else would make a man confess to a crime thirteen years after it happened? Such was the case of Gary Kerpan, a forty-year-old resident of Spartanburg, South Carolina. Kerpan called the FBI one morning in 1990 to confess to the 1977 murder of a twelve-year-old girl in Waukegan, Illinois. He had truly gotten away with the crime. But his conscience would not let him be at peace with himself.

This is part of the biblical truth we present to prisoners in prison ministry—that we can repent, and God can forgive us, but we must pay our debt to society. Criminals are accountable. The message we must bring to the church and society in general is the same, but with different emphasis. That message is: We are all the same, all sinners. We must all be held accountable for what we do. But we can all come to the Lord for forgiveness. And then we must reach out to others who need both accountability and forgiveness.

From time to time in our country, we have all seen examples of powerful people proclaiming one standard but living by another. Remember the videotape of Washington, D.C. mayor Marion Barry handing money to a woman for crack cocaine, then putting the substance in a smoking apparatus and smoking it? Or what about the news of a famous televangelist who fell into crime and immorality and was sentenced to a federal prison?

No one, not even the most respected or the most notorious, is immune to sin or incapable of redemption. Our prisons, after all, hold not just people who were born on the "wrong side of the tracks," but people in every station of life. I meet prisoners who came from the ghetto, who were involved in street gangs, who were down-and-out drug abusers. But I also meet prisoners who were lawyers and judges, police officers, stock traders, corporation executives, and—lamentably—ministers and church leaders.

Mother York has said the beginning of understanding justice is the reality that we in the free world are really no different from those in prison. As she says, "There are only two categories of folk—the caught and the uncaught. We just didn't get caught. We haven't had justice measured out, or we would be dead and in hell ourselves, certainly in prison." She adds emphatically,

"Without God's grace, without the blood of Christ to cover our sins, we are all wretched and unworthy."

I believe the future of prison ministry will be bright as churches come to realize that God's mercy is the only thing that separates their congregation from being on the other side of prison walls.

11

God's Minimum Standard for Jail and Prison Ministry Volunteers

Harry L. Greene

Through the chaplains of Harry Greene's Good News Jail and Prison Ministry, more than 94,000 decisions for Christ have been made in thirty years. Out of his experience, and relying on the text of Philippians 4, Mr. Greene spells out a set of minimum standards for every phase of jail and prison ministry. He begins by saying that prayer is central to everything. We must pray that God's power will work through the ministry and that his agenda will be accomplished. Then, if ministries are to have significant impact on the prisons and the local church, they need to show by example that they can work together. That means practicing the peace of God by building one another up instead of criticizing one another.

Mr. Greene uses Philippians 4:8 to demonstrate the central features of his appeal for standards by saying that ministries must be true, which means reliable and truthworthy; they must be noble, or worthy of respect; and they must be right, pure, lovely, and admirable. He concludes that the most important standard for each and every jail and prison ministry is to be faithful to God's call.

All of us who minister within the criminal justice system work within structured, regulated environments. The American Correctional Association, the American Jail Association, the National Sheriffs Association all have espoused minimum standards of operations and base their performance on those guidelines.

As jail and prison ministers, we also need standards. And we *have* standards; God has given them to us. There are many throughout Scripture and they are indeed varied, useful, and certainly applicable. I want to concentrate on Philippians 4, which I believe is one of the most powerful, compelling exhortations in Scripture.

A Policy of Rejoicing

While the primary verses that I want to focus on are 8 and 9, we can begin back in verse 4 where Paul says, "Rejoice in the Lord, always. I will say it again: Rejoice!" Twice he tells us to rejoice.

Notice that he does *not* tell us to be happy. I don't think Paul's circumstances were very happy at this time; he was in prison. And yet he chose an attitude of rejoicing. Today we have a problem in that too many ministers of the gospel are looking to be happy in their ministry rather than rejoicing in their ministry.

More importantly, Paul tells us to "rejoice *in the Lord*" (emphasis added). We need to be dwellers on the positives, not letting ourselves be dragged down by negatives. For example, we could hear a weather report that says there is a 30 percent chance of rain and immediately think we have to cancel the picnic, forgetting that we have a 70 percent chance of sunshine. While I do not believe in false optimism nor overly rosy outlooks, I do believe that if we rejoice in the Lord, as he has commanded us to do, we *will* see something happen. God will meet our needs. Our attitudes, our relationships to God and others will be what they should be. And we will find out one other thing—that rejoicing is contagious.

Paul goes on to say, "Let your gentleness be evident to all" (v. 5). What he is saying there translates to being forebearing, having a nonretaliatory spirit. We are to be of good temper, known to all men by how we live. Do you ever feel that you minister in a fishbowl? Do you ever feel that everyone—inmate, staff, correctional system—is watching you, just waiting for you to make a mistake? Well, Paul says we are to live in such a way that the fishbowl isn't a problem.

What we are talking about here is integrity. Does your ministry have integrity? There are many definitions of the word *integrity*. I believe the best one simply says, "Integrity is what we do when no one sees us."

People of Prayer

Paul then goes on to say: "Do not be anxious about anything, but in everything, by prayer and petition, with thanksgiving, present your requests to God" (v. 6). This verse echoes what Matthew 6:25 says about anxiety—that we are not to be worried or anxious, that God will supply. But I believe that the main focus of this verse is prayer. Prayer is the foundation of our personal lives in the ministry of the church, and if it isn't, then it certainly should be. I think of Nehemiah and the task of rebuilding the walls of Jerusalem. As we read through the Book of Nehemiah, we find that before Nehemiah acted, before he did anything, he prayed. We, too, more than ever before in the history of our ministries, need to be men and women of prayer. If we are to see ministry go forward in jails and prisons, we will see it from a kneeling position!

You know, it is hard to find time to pray. I don't know about you, but time management is one of our organization's biggest struggles. The day can be all planned out, then something comes along and upsets it, and suddenly we are cast into a mode that we had not even thought about that day. We are called upon to do things which were not on our schedule, things which certainly inhibit us, and in some cases actually restrict us, from doing the things we had planned to do. This causes concern and anxiety, and this is why, more than ever, we need to be much in prayer.

When we examine the earthly ministry of our Lord, we find that he was fervent in prayer and relaxed in ministry. He could sit and feed thousands, and minister to thousands, yet his intense moments came when he was in prayer. We tend to turn that pattern around; we are fervent in ministry and relaxed in prayer.

And that's when we get in trouble. I believe that we need to be men and women of prayer and that we need to be as James was known. They called him "old camel knees" because he spent so much time there.

The Peace that Changes Everything

Paul goes on in verse 7 to talk about "the peace of God." This peace is extremely hard to explain and almost beyond comprehension; it "transcends all understanding." It comes as a result of the prayerful attitude talked about in verse 6. It reassures us and comforts us. It "guards our hearts and our minds in Christ Jesus." That word translated "guard" is actually a military term. It refers to a soldier's assignment to watch over a certain area. And God's power does watch over us, doesn't it? There is no way that you or I or anyone who is in jail and prison ministry could claim any success without the power of God, without the peace of God. What else enables us to go into a jail or a prison, to look a man or a woman in the eye and tell him or her about the love of Jesus Christ without a false agenda, without undue credit to ourselves? It is simply the love of God, the peace of God, that enables us to do that.

One result of this peace of God is better relationships within the institutions. If I am at peace with God, I am probably at peace with other people. The peace of God should help me to have a servant's heart, the right work ethic, the right attitude, and the right professionalism—not from a secular standpoint, but from a biblical one.

The peace of God also helps me avoid gossip and rumors. I believe that gossip is one of the tools that the devil uses the most in this world today. If he can get us talking about one another, criticizing one another, envying one another, then what has he accomplished? He has taken us away from focusing on God. To anyone who comes to me and begins to criticize another ministry or to confront me with gossip, rumor, and innuendo, I would say, I don't want to hear it! What I would prefer to hear is what God is doing in your ministry. What are you rejoicing about? What is the result of the blessing of God within your work?

Let's not downplay and downgrade another! That's not what God's peace is about. In fact, the peace of God has exactly the opposite effect. It results in harmony; it results in love. So if someone comes to us and talks about what God is doing in their ministry, let us not be envious. And let us not be ashamed of what God is doing within our own ministry. Instead, let us rejoice together. Let us have a harmony and a love for one another, a peace with one another that enables us to go forward together in a field that is desperately crying for more workers.

Six Words to Revolutionize a Ministry

We come now to verses 8 and 9 of Philippians 4. When Paul wrote this, as the Holy Spirit moved him to write it, I believe that he probably pondered greatly. I don't see Paul in any way as a braggart, an egotist, or a man who set himself above others. In fact, the opposite is true. And yet here, God's Spirit moves Paul to write, "Whatever you have learned or received or heard from me, or seen in me—put it into practice" (v. 9). In other words, Paul is saying, "Act like me; I am your example."

Just what kind of life does Paul want us to emulate? He sums it up in verse 8: "Finally, brothers, whatever is right, whatever is pure, whatever is lovely, whatever is admirable—if anything is excellent or praiseworthy—think about such things."

Let's look together at six words Paul uses in this verse. If we take the time to really study these words, to really think upon them, to pray about them, and to apply them in our lives, then I believe we can expect God to revolutionize our ministry. I believe we can expect him to raise up to a level of service we cannot even begin to comprehend.

Whatever Is True

The first word in verse 8 that I want to examine is *true*. The word translated here means honest, reliable, trustworthy. What an important standard to start out with! After all, nothing we do or say means much without it. I have seen again and again in our ministry that the chaplains who have the most difficulty or who fail are the ones who have the most problem in this area. So if we want our ministry to move forward, we need to ask ourselves some pointed questions.

First, are we honest? In any of our relationships—with people in our organization, with God, with our families, even with ourselves—we are in for a difficult time if we cannot face truth and speak truth.

And are we reliable? Can people count on us? Can we be relied upon to do the right thing?

Are we trustworthy? Can people place their trust in us and not have any doubt as to our ability to merit it or maintain it?

What powerful words *honest, reliable,* and *trustworthy* are. And they all come together in that simple word *true.*

Whatever Is Noble

The second important word in Philippians 4:8 is *noble.* The translation here is "dignified." "Worthy of respect" might be another way of looking at it. Are you and I worthy of respect from those to whom we minister and those with whom we work within this system we call corrections?

One of the biggest challenges for a volunteer or a chaplain or anyone else in prison ministry is to walk the line between having inmates trust you and the corrections staff respect you. To be worthy of respect, you must walk the talk. You must maintain that dignified, professional, committed attitude that says, I am a servant of the Lord Jesus Christ, and I want everything I do and say to reflect my love for him and my servanthood for him. That's a difficult position, a difficult thing to do. And yet that's what we must strive for daily so that we might in no way be hypocritical, that we might in no way cast doubt upon the gospel we preach.

I am reminded of a director of corrections who came to Christ and then told one of our chaplains, "One of the reasons that I came to a point where I began to search my own heart as to my relationship with God was the respect that I have for you. For eight years I have seen you walk the talk, knowing that there had to be something real in what you were saying." We all need to be that kind of example. We need to have that kind of nobility.

Whatever Is Right

The next word is *right*—some translations render it *just*. It refers to conformity to God's standard or to God's Word. I cannot stress this idea enough. We need to be righteous. We need to be right before God and before man. And when we become aware that we are not doing right and being right, we need to take scriptural steps to remedy the situation.

I am appalled at the number of people in ministry who feel they don't have to worry about such things as accountability and responsibility, about doing the right thing and setting the right example. In fact, we who are in ministry are called to a higher standard of righteousness than others. We need to pay special attention to doing right and being righteous.

I am also very concerned about the competitive spirit that exists between some prison ministry organizations. Instead of striving after God's standards of righteousness and accepting his blessings gratefully, we feel we have to beat the other guy. It is true that ministries do seek support from the same churches and individuals, but God has provided more than enough for all of us if we would but let him do with us what he wishes and then give him the glory.

Whatever Is Pure

This next word is one of the most difficult to live up to: *pure*. It means wholesome, good for us, not tainted.

You and I live today in a society whose values have become tainted. We work in a system that is far from wholesome. We deal on a daily basis with people who society has said are no good— throw away the key, lock them up? And yet Paul tells us to be pure, to be wholesome.

How can we be wholesome in a world that is doing everything it can to pull us down? We do it by maintaining these standards that we are talking about. We do it by not placing ourselves in positions that we can be criticized for or even to be ejected from a jail. One of our chaplains recently, for reasons known only to himself, chose to breach the security of his institution. He was trying, in his opinion, to help some inmates. And yet he knowingly and willingly broke that institution's rules. He paid a heavy price when that institution said to him, "You can no longer minister here." And our organization had to go along with that decision.

We must not be tainted. We must do what is good for us, for the ministry, for the spreading of the gospel. And we must do what is wholesome. You know, *wholesome* is a word that has almost become passé, and yet it is certainly applicable to all of us today. If we are going to minister the Word of God, we need to be as wholesome as we can be. We can never be perfect, but we can strive to be pure and honest in our thoughts, our attitudes, our desires, and—most importantly—our motivations.

May I say to you that in the thirty-year history of Good News Jail and Prison Ministry, not one inmate was ever saved by a chaplain? God does that! In the last four years, our chaplains have reported 94,000 decisions for Christ. And those decisions were not just raised hands. Those decisions were not the same individual getting saved six times on different days. Those decisions were reported only after there was evidence of change in a life.

We are not trying to be judgmental. But you and I know that we minister in an environment that is less than honest. We know there are inmates that go into court with a Bible in their hand and a cross around their neck saying, "Hallelujah! Praise God! I've changed" and expect the judge to cut them some slack. So what we look for is some evidence of change—a difference in attitude, demeanor, speech, or personality—before we report a decision. Again, we are not being judgmental. If an individual never indicates any change and yet has truly accepted Christ, we know he will spend eternity with all of us. And we thank God for every decision, as I know that you do.

Let's be pure. Let's be wholesome. Let's do what is good for us. Let's not be tainted. And especially, let's not have our ministry be tainted.

Whatever Is Lovely

The last two words are found only in this one verse of the New Testament. First is the word *lovely,* which in the Greek means to promote peace rather than conflict. I love that idea. After all, what does a chaplain do? Time and again, our chaplains promote peace rather than conflict.

So many sheriffs and wardens and superintendents across the country have told me that the chaplain brings down the temperature or the volatility of the institution. And he does it just by his presence, just by being someone whom both staff and people can talk to and appreciate.

We in ministry must strive to be lovely people. If we are venting our anger, if we are making light or sport of another ministry, what are we saying? Are we being lovely? For that matter, are we being pure, just, noble, or true? I would have to say that we are not.

"Turn the other cheek," "Love one another as I have loved you," "Do unto others as you would have them do unto you"— all of these are standards, aren't they? And yet they could be described in this one word. Let us be lovely people.

Whatever Is Admirable

Last, Paul talks about being *admirable,* or being of good report. This word means to be positive and constructive instead of negative and destructive. I believe the greatest force we have for the Lord today is the collective power of the church to move toward evangelism, discipleship, training, and all of those things we know to be right. But I believe one of the greatest tools of the devil is also found in the power of the church—or should I say the *lack* of power in the church.

You and I know that the Great Commission was not given to your ministry nor mine, but to the church as a whole. And we need to do all we can to be positive and constructive and allow the church to fulfill that Great Commission. There are enough negative things being said about ministers, ministries, and churches today. In contrast, we need to be positive—not with a false sense of euphoria, but with an attitude that says Jesus Christ makes the difference.

God has given us the opportunity to serve, to share, to tell others of this Good News that is available to them. We need to pursue this opportunity in the most powerfully and constructive and positive way that we can. That means we avoid negative and destructive actions. We don't criticize others or accuse them falsely. And we don't become so wrapped up in feeling wronged or unappreciated that we take God right out of the equation.

Think about It

True, noble, right, pure, lovely, and *admirable*—these six words give us God's minimum standards for jail and prison ministry. If we are to be the ministers we want to be, if we want to spread the gospel of Jesus Christ and see men and women and young people behind bars come to know him, then we need to realize how true these words must be in our own lives. We need to walk this talk.

At the end of verse 8, Paul says something extremely important: "Think about such things." Other translations say "dwell upon" or "meditate on." Most of us today do very little thinking or meditating. We act, but we don't really plan. We have little idea where we are going or what is truly important to us. And then we wonder why our ministries do not succeed.

"Think about these things." If you and I take the time to do that, I believe we will see that we are really examining ourselves. We are also assessing how others view us. That kind of self-analysis can be painful, but it helps us grow.

When we "think about these things," we are also doing a priority check. We know our priorities are supposed to be God, family, and ministry. And yet how many of us can truthfully say that our ministry has not supplanted family or even God in our hearts?

Taking the time to "think on these things" also means evaluating our stewardship of time, talent, and treasure. You and I, as ministers of the gospel of Jesus Christ, must realize the importance of these standards we have just looked at. We must be measured in light of them.

Certified and Approved

The correction institutions where we work must adhere to minimum standards of operations. Inspectors periodically come and do an audit for certification of those facilities, and they must prove beyond doubt that they stand up to the test. If those inspectors came to you and me, would we be able to stand up to the test? If they audited our performance in light of God's minimum standards, would we receive certification?

You and I need to do all we can to meet these standards so that our ministries might be what we would have them be for God and that we might see the results. And we will measure those results not only in changed lives, but in our influence on those who follow after us. We need to be able to say, "These things that you have seen me do in this ministry, in this jail, or in this prison—these are the things you need to do. This is the way that you can minister successfully, and this is what God will bless."

There is a magnificent Christian song that says, "May those who follow after find us faithful." That is a good word for us. May we preserve the ministry God has given so that when we do have the opportunity to pass on to others the great torch of jail and prison ministry, those who receive it from our hand won't have to go back and worry about relighting the flame. May they be able to see it burn brighter because of our efforts. And may those who receive it from us look upon us as we must look upon the apostle Paul and say, "Well done, good and faithful servant. You stayed the course. You did the best you could. But more importantly, your ministry was a beacon that loudly proclaimed the standards God has set."

May we go forward more determined than ever before that when that audit happens, those who do the certification will stamp in large letters, "Approved, worthy servant of the Lord Jesus Christ."

12

A Matter of Perspective

Don Smarto

In this chapter, the editor explores the question of perspective. He admits early in the chapter that the transformation of offenders by the grace and power of God is something the world will never understand. No matter how powerful the conversions of ex-offenders can be, some people will never see it or will refuse to see it. Such selective blindness, he says, is consistent with the Scriptures. So he suggests that prison ministry should not be concerned with the press and secular opinions but, as Harry Greene said in the previous chapter, should strive for faithfulness.

The editor further shows that jail and prison ministry is a great sign to the church in showing that no one is beyond God's mercy, that God is acting as powerfully today as he did in biblical times, and that it is really the church's responsibility, not that of government, to reach out to prisoners. In response to that sign, he says, we must be in constant prayer for inmates, hold out the lordship of Christ as the only solution, and become personally involved through volunteerism. We do not have to make broad gestures or claim great numbers to accomplish much in this ministry. Through personal examples, he shows that it is often the little things people do that impact on human hearts. Therein lies the great power of prison ministry for now and for the future.

How we view prison ministry is really a matter of perspective. If you ask people on the street, at random, "What do you really think about ministry to prisoners?" how many would say it is important or worthwhile? How many would actually want to become involved? Half? More than half? Less than half?

You are probably thinking that it depends on *who* you ask.

Okay, let's make a change. Let's ask only Christians, who surely will endorse ministry to prisoners. If we ask every Christian in America, how many would be enthusiastic?

Again you are probably saying, "It depends on *which* Christians you are asking."

Those of us who are in the prison ministry field, out on the frontlines, know that this ministry gets mixed reviews. Some people are skeptical. Others are apprehensive. Sure, it's mandated in the Bible. But don't you know of other biblical mandates that are ignored? Don't you know of other biblical mandates to which people are slow to respond or even disobedient? So we might ask, Is it important for the masses to applaud prison ministry with enthusiasm?

I'm going to suggest to you that our labors will *always* get mixed reviews. The press accentuates crime, not rehabilitation. Prison reform is traditionally unpopular in the political arena. Public opinion polls reveal a desire for harsher punishments. The courts concentrate on revenge rather than restoration.

So who is the staunch advocate for the offender's reformation? It should be the responsibility and mandate of the church. I have long believed that jail and prison ministry is a great sign to the church today—a sign that speaks to us in three ways:

1. Prison ministry shows the church that no one is beyond God's mercy.
2. Prison ministry demonstrates that God is acting as powerfully today as he did in biblical times.
3. Jail and prison ministry is a great sign that working with prisoners is not an elective for the local church.

It's a great sign, but not universally seen. People have to *want* to see—and some things are difficult to make out.

A Matter of Perspective

In the late fifties and early sixties, the late Fritz Reiner was conductor of the Chicago Symphony Orchestra. Reiner was not known for his exuberance. He didn't have what I would call the gusto or the broad gestures of, let's say, a Leonard Bernstein. His conducting style was very reserved; a one-inch movement of his baton could mean the difference between piano and fortissimo. And this could mean problems for the instrumentalists in the back of the orchestra, who had trouble seeing what he wanted.

One day, as a joke, one of the string bass players brought a telescope on a tripod. As he played, he peered through the telescope. At a certain point, Fritz Reiner saw the telescope and stopped. He got out a pen and scrawled something on a tiny piece of paper—only about an inch square. Reiner held up the little piece of paper toward the string bass player. The player could not read it with the naked eye, so he looked at it through his telescope. It said, "You're fired!"

This is a case of a different perspective, the bass player thought his act was clever and funny. But Reiner saw it differently.

There is a man in the Philippines who finds great amusement in showing tourists a particular monument that commemorates the death of the Portuguese explorer, Magellen. The inscription reads, "Here on the 27th of April, 1521, the great navigator Magellen was slain in service to the King of Spain." However, if you go to the other side of the monument, there is a different inscription: "Here on the 27th of April, 1527, the great chieftain Lapu Lapu repelled an attack by Spaniards, sending the forces away." One side of the monument memorializes a European tragedy; the other side celebrates an Oriental triumph.

Two sides of one monument. Two perspectives. The point is this: two people can witness the same event and yet not see the same thing. We know this to be true from courtroom testimony. What a witness observes is partially based upon his or her interpretation, expectations, and predispositions. Witnesses often disagree and contradict each other in court.

Perception is not merely a matter of sight, but also discernment. There is a problem right now with the security system in a federal building in downtown Chicago. Well, the head of security doesn't think it is a problem, but most everybody who comes into the building does. It seems that every article placed on the conveyor belt of the X-ray machine runs off the belt. Everyone's briefcase falls on the floor. When quizzed about this recently, the head of security said defensively, "Any bombs not detected by X-ray explode harmlessly when the briefcase hits the floor."

It really is possible for different people to have totally different perspectives on the same reality. One astronomer looks out to the heavens and sees order, harmony, and the imprint of the Creator. Another astronomer looks out at the same sky and sees an accident, chance, no plan at all.

In 1988 the editors of *Life* magazine asked three hundred people this question: "What is the meaning of life?" They asked poets, scientists, artists, politicians, philosophers, manual laborers. Responses came in from widely differing sources—from Bertrand Russell to convict 79206 in Sing Sing, from Ted Turner to Billy Graham. The contrasting answers should not surprise us.

One answer to the question was: "The meaning of life is the development of our social structures. There is perhaps a force but it is unknown to us." That was written by a current U.S. Supreme Court justice.

Another response said, "There is no grand overall design. There is no master plan. It's all random. I don't believe in God." That was from a New York City homicide detective.

And here is a third one: "Humanity is not an accident. Life has profound meaning. God deliberately put us here and endowed us with a spiritual nature." That was Billy Graham's response.

Not Everyone Sees It

People do not see the same thing even when looking at the same thing. In Jesus, some saw God incarnate, the Good Shepherd, the Savior. Others, looking at the same person, saw a lunatic a rebel, even a demon. The same Man was loved by some, feared and shunned by others. If people looking at Jesus, seeing the same man, seeing the same activities, hearing the same message, witnessing the same miracles, came to such radically different conclusions about him, why should we be surprised that prison ministry has such mixed reviews?

Some say, "Prison ministry is great! It gives the church an opportunity to minister to men and women whom God loves." Others say, "It's a great sign of God's power and mercy. What a wonderful blessing of transformed lives!" And yet others say, in essence, that prison ministry just isn't very important. Some ask questions like, "How can you be sure criminals have really changed?" Some say, "Well, it's all right—but not in my community. Not in my church."

I have been personally blessed by this ministry. Some of my most dynamic worship experiences have occurred in jails and prisons. I have met dedicated, selfless chaplains, volunteers who sacrifice much, and correctional workers who are professional and godly. I have seen lives dramatically changed. But it would be far too simplistic for me to assume that everyone sees this.

To see prison ministry properly, I believe we must look at the poor and hurting people as Jesus did. There are really two definitions of the word *see*. One is "to look at, to recognize what is literally there." But there is another definition. To see also means "to believe what is possible, to imagine, to see potential." And that's how Jesus responded to the people he met.

The account of the calling of Matthew the tax collector is recorded in three of the Gospels. Basically, Matthew was a cheat. But he invited Jesus into his house, and Jesus had no problem accepting the invitation. The Gospels record that some of the guests at Matthew's home were notorious swindlers, notorious sinners. The Pharisees and the teachers of the law merely saw the thieves and cheats, so they called the disciples aside and asked, to quote the Living Bible paraphrase, "How can he stand it, to eat with such scum?" (Mark 2:16 LB). Jesus saw the sinners, too, but he knew they needed to hear his message. He knew that they could change. He said to the religious leaders in response, "Sick people need a doctor, not healthy ones" (v. 17).

Jesus sees in every sinner a potential saint. When the prostitute was thrown in front of Jesus, Jesus saw something in her that no one else saw. Everyone in the crowd was looking for condemnation, even possible execution, yet Jesus saw her potential.

Dwight Moody was a great evangelist who sought to reach a mass of people who actually never went to church. It is said that Moody traveled a million miles and spoke to a million people, yet he had no college or seminary education. He liked to be thought of as "the gap man," the person who filled in the gap between the clergy and ordinary people. But his critics called him "Crazy Moody" because he went into the saloons and back alleys and met with hoodlums and beggars and street urchins. What did Moody see that others did not see? What did he believe was possible? What did he imagine looking into the faces of hoodlums and beggars and urchins? He saw the potential of sinners transformed by God's grace. Moody had hope in his heart, and he brought a message of hope for society's outcasts and rejects. Ministry to prisoners is like Dwight Moody's ministry, a great sign to the church. But again, not everyone sees that fact.

While in Washington, D.C. recently, I visited the National Gallery of Art. I spent some time gazing at Salvador Dali's massive canvas, "Last Supper." After looking at the painting for a while, I suddenly noticed something I had never seen before—an image of a dove in Jesus' hair. The artist intended that dove to be there. It's a symbol of the Holy Spirit, a clue of a metaphysical reality. But I am sure many people look at the painting every day and never see it.

While still in Washington, I also went to the United States Capitol building and saw another very famous painting, one we have all seen in our history books—the large portrait of the signing of the Declaration of Independence. And the tour guide pointed out something about that painting I had never seen, although I had seen that picture many times over the years. Thomas Jefferson is standing next to Aaron Burr. These two men didn't like each other in real life. And in the picture, under the table, Thomas Jefferson is stepping on Aaron Burr's foot. The artist meant that partly as humor, partly as a comment on the relationship. Now that it was pointed out to me, I'll always see it.

As in that painting, there are realities we must point out to the church, things we must show them. And once they see it, I hope,

they'll always see it. The changed life of offenders is a great sign
of God's power and mercy.

God's Signature

The definition of *sign* is "something that suggests the presence
or existence of a fact." It can also mean "to write one's signature."
And God's signature is written all over jail and prison ministry. It
says, "My love extends far beyond the limits of human judgment
and prejudice." It is a great sign to the church today that says,
"Your God is merciful even to the rejected, the scorned, the de-
spised, and those who you have thrown out."

The New Testament records the story of a man who was literally rejected by a whole town; it is told in Matthew 8, Mark 5, and
Luke 8. Jesus took a boat across a lake to visit this man. He was
wild—a crazy person. He lived in a cemetery. At night the townspeople heard his screams. He was naked and homeless.

What did the townspeople see in this man? They saw a man
beyond hope, an animal that needed handcuffs and shackles. But
Jesus healed him, and the demonic spirits that possessed this man
were sent into a herd of pigs that plunged headlong off a cliff and
into the waters. The people of the town rushed to see what was
happening. And no, they did not see a crazed animal, but they
saw a man sitting quietly, "dressed and in his right mind" (Luke
8:35).

Were these people happy to have Jesus with them? Were they
excited about his power and his compassion and his healing?
You're laughing to yourself because you know that isn't what
they were saying or thinking. No, the townspeople begged Jesus
to go, to leave them alone. And they were not astounded by the
transformation of a man. They were more concerned about the
loss of a herd of pigs.

Only a simplistic and erroneous view of the gospel would conclude that all are attracted by the power and truth of Jesus. Members of his own family were embarrassed by him. A whole town
begged him to go away. In fact, according to John 6:66, "many
disciples turned back and no longer followed him." They did not
get what they were expecting. They didn't get the earthly power
now that they wanted. They came to understand that following

Jesus wasn't going to be fun every minute along the way, and so they deserted him.

When that happened, Jesus turned to his disciples and asked, "You do not want to leave too, do you?" Peter answered, "Lord, to whom shall we go?" (vv. 67, 68). In a sense, Peter was giving us the answer to the question *Life* magazine asked: "What is the meaning of life?" Peter's statement answered, "Jesus." And of course, that is the key to prison ministry as well. We don't change prisoners through behavior modification. We don't change them through more prison construction. We don't change them through more psychology. Prisoners' lives change through the saving blood of Jesus Christ!

In Sacramento, California, I saw another painting whose symbolism seems especially appropriate for prison ministry. The painting, which was done in 1640, depicts a shipwreck. The ship was sinking, and some people were trying to swim for their lives and crying out for help. But the interesting part of the painting was in the foreground—three people standing on the deck. One person had his head bowed and was praying. The second person was holding high a cross. And the third person was kneeling at the edge of the water, trying to grab people with his hand.

That's a superb model for ministry. We must first commit ourselves to constant prayer because it's always God's power working through us. We must never be apologetic that we are under the lordship and banner of Christ. And we must become personally involved, extending an outstretched hand.

Some people will never be effective in ministry because they don't want to enter the world of troubled people. They don't want to get messy. They don't want to get cold. They don't want to get wet. But that third man was literally on the edge of the water, grasping for people. We must do that. We must *pray*. We must hold up the *banner of Christ,* but we must also *enter* the sometimes chilly *world of people who are hurting.*

Several months ago I spoke in a church. After my message, the pastor gave an invitation. As I sat there with my eyes closed, I heard one of the most plaintive cries that has ever come to my ears. A woman had come forward and was repeatedly crying out, "Jesus, save me! Jesus, save me!" If I had not known I was in a church, I would have thought someone was drowning. Those cries sounded like they came from someone gasping with her last breath, yelling to be saved before being clutched by the jaws of death. I can hear her voice even now in my head because of the sincerity and helplessness of that anguished cry. We are so polite, so quiet in our suburban churches. But that woman didn't care what anyone thought. She just knew two things—that she was drowning, and that she needed a savior. Many prisoners feel that way today. And I think drowning people see Jesus a lot better than people who are comfortable and satisfied and content.

Public Relations Is Not the Point

I've often wondered what reporters would have covered if they had lived in Jesus' day. What events would have struck them as newsworthy? I am convinced that the press would have ignored Jesus' calling of the disciples. But they certainly would have covered the suicide of Judas; that would have been good for the front page of the *National Enquirer,* with a graphic photo.

They certainly would have put in a headline, "Jesus Dies on Cross." They would be in a hurry to cover an execution, just as today's press is appealing to the state of California to show a man being executed in the gas chamber. Death makes good copy; it sells. Then, somewhere on the eighth page, in a very small column, you might find, reported as a fantasy, the rumor of a resurrection.

I think somebody would have wanted to interview Saul the persecutor. Anger and hatred—as in crosses burning on lawns—always make good copy. But the press would have dismissed Paul's conversion as religious delusion. They would have wanted to report the details of Peter's denial. That would be good for *Hard Copy* or *Entertainment Tonight.* But the maturity of a growing Peter and his church leadership—that would be bad for the ratings.

Is the press different today? News is still sensational. Murder is news but not the transformation of the murderer. Murder is news, but not a murderer who becomes a productive, law-abiding citizen. I am convinced that a ministry to prisoners is at best a curiosity to the secular press whose eyes are always searching for parole violators and guilty verdicts and violent crimes, but do not see healing, reconciliation, restoration, and restitution.

I was recently interviewed by the *Chicago Tribune*. The reporter kept asking me, "How can you be sure prisoners who make a decision for Christ have really changed; how do you know they are not faking?" When that interview came out in the newspaper, I wasn't surprised that the headline read "Prison ministries *say* they save souls." The secular press is more interested in the jewel thief "Murph the Surf" than they are in the evangelist Jack Murphy. They are more interested in Colson the hatchet man than in Colson the leader of a great prison-ministry movement. They are more interested in a mad dog than a domesticated creature. It's no surprise. And you know what, I don't think it matters. I don't really think our job is to convince society. I don't think our job is to turn around public opinion. I don't think our job is to convert the secular press. I think our job is to be *faithful!* Our job is to minister to those who are hurt and neglected. Our job is to give the prisoner an opportunity for change. Who cares what the secular press thinks? I don't.

It was said in the Bible that even if someone comes back from the dead, many will refuse to believe. And guess what? Someone *did* come back from the dead, and they *do* refuse to believe.

What Counts in Ministry

The things we do in ministry don't have to be large or flamboyant in order to have impact. They don't have to have the gestures of a Leonard Bernstein; they can have the small, reserved gestures of a Fritz Reiner. In fact, it's the little things we do that the prisoners really see, even when we don't know they are watching.

A woman I met many years ago, Mrs. Rinaldo, made a big impression on me. I met her every day in my high school cafeteria where she worked in the serving line. One of the things that impressed me about this woman was her broad, infectious smile. She made me feel good every day as I went through that cafeteria line. She was kind to me, and she was also very generous. I was a rather shy, gawky, high-school freshman, and I usually didn't have much lunch money. At best I could come up with a quarter, and all you could get in the school cafeteria line for a quarter was a scoop of mashed potatoes with some gravy. She'd always be extra generous with those potatoes. As she smiled and gave me my food, she'd always say, "Good to see you." It was such a simple act of service—just a smile and a word and a scoop of potatoes. But every day Mrs. Rinaldo affirmed me. The little things we do for the lost, the poor, the hurting really have a great impact.

I have said, especially when I speak to chaplains, that the experiences God uses most as he prepares us for ministry are often not the ones we expect. A lot of people in ministry have been prepared by the twists and turns and turmoil of life.

It may seem like a paradox, but God can use your moments of weakness. God can use your sense of helplessness. God can use your sense of inadequacy. God can use your knowledge of your limitations, your awareness of your own rebellion and sin. I know there's a school out there that argues rather convincingly that the keys to success are social skills, charm, education, the gathering of accolades, and the approval of peers. If we have swallowed that line, let me suggest that we have it backwards. If we watch how God used Gideon and David and Peter, we will begin to realize he can use anyone—yes, anyone—who trusts him, and God prefers to build strength and leadership on a foundation of weakness and brokenness.

There have been days when I believe I am in control, when I think the good things that happen in ministry are due to my own efforts. For those days God has planted in my head an image from the past—and I thank God for it. I remember a three-story frame house in Chicago that my wife and I lived in five times over the last nine years—though not by choice. That house left an indelible impression in my mind. It's called the Ronald McDonald House, but don't let the images of clowns fool you. It's a home away from home for parents of very sick children—children dying of cancer, children struggling for life in intensive care.

I never expected to have a son dying of heart failure. No one does. Sometimes during those agonizing times I remember thinking, *This isn't fair.* Some years earlier, I had been studying in a monastery, committed to celibacy. Then my life took a wonderful turn. Suddenly I had a Christian wife, a beautiful baby boy. God was just so good. Then, just as suddenly, tests revealed that our son needed open-heart surgery, then a second open-heart surgery, then a third open-heart surgery. And all this time we would be living in this Ronald McDonald House, sharing our fears with other parents of sick children. The thin walls often betrayed the grief of those in the next room.

There are not many moments in life as agonizing as those spent watching a suffering child. I'll admit to you that there were times that I questioned God and I felt helpless. I felt I had no control over the situation. I felt broken. There were times I felt utterly dependent on God's grace. And that's probably just where God wanted me.

My friends, if as a leader you are depending on your own intelligence and resourcefulness, if you think you are in control, think again. Consider that it is out of your brokenness, not your strength, that God's power works through you.

A Matter of Faithfulness

Oswald Chambers once said, "The destined end of man is not happiness, not health, but holiness." Another way of saying that would be that the destined end of man is not success, but faithfulness. The goal of a Christian is not power, but servanthood. The great thing is that God chooses to use us at all in ministry. He didn't have to build us into the plan. But he did. And he called us to be faithful, period.

Someone once said perseverance, like faith, is the gift of God. To me, jail and prison ministry epitomizes perseverance. You'll not always receive recognition in the local community. You'll not always even receive recognition from your own church. At times you'll be manipulated by prisoners. You will have painful experiences. But take heart; God will not abandon you.

About a year ago, a church near Wheaton College burned to the ground. The congregation rebuilt it. When they had the opening ceremonies of the new church, the minister said, "This is not a celebration of what we did; rather, it is a celebration of what God did through us. We had to go through significant changes in the church. We had to change from our comfortable attitude to a faith-oriented, adventuresome attitude."

This is not a ministry for those who want to play it safe. This is a ministry for those who are willing to step out in faith and leave the comfort zone. "We conquer by continuing," someone once said. And Eleanor Roosevelt once said this: "You gain strength, courage and confidence by every experience in which you really stop to look fear in the face. You were able to say to yourself, I lived through this horror, I can take the next thing that comes along. You must do the thing you think you cannot do."

Mrs. Rinaldo's acts of kindness impressed me when I was a high-school freshman. But what really impressed me was learning, during the last week of my freshman year, that she had died of inoperable cancer. All that time I saw her being generous and smiling, she knew she was dying. She was in pain. But she obviously made a conscious, deliberate choice to reject self-sympathy. She made a choice not to focus on her own pain, but instead to turn to others in service. Her smile was purposeful. And it's clear that her simple acts of kindness made a powerful impact on a young boy, because here I am, thirty-one years later, writing about her.

The little things we do make a difference. Offer friendship to a lonely prisoner, be kind to a man or woman whom others think is beyond hope. The change may not be seen tomorrow. It may not be your actions alone that melt a hardened heart, but the effect of many people coming to minister to that person. But the "crazy man who lives among the tombs" can someday become a man of peace, gentle and transformed. Allow God to use you, in spite of public opinion, in spite of skeptics. Do not worry about being heroic; just be faithful.

Meeting People's Needs

Many times while my son was recovering from one of those surgeries, I would drive forty miles home and find a little box with bread and canned goods by the front door. One day I found an envelope in our mailbox with two hundred dollars in it from an anonymous friend. I needed those things, but I had never asked for them.

Don't wait for people to make a plea. See them with the eyes of Jesus. There are people all around us who are hurting. There are people who are lonely and just need someone to listen to them. There are people all around us with fears and doubts, who need encouragement.

The identification with hurting people we see Jesus articulating in Matthew 25 means meeting people's most elementary needs. You see those who are hungry, and you feed them. You see those who are cold, and you give them a coat or a blanket. You see those who are lonely, and you visit them. It's that simple. And regarding prisoners, notice that Matthew 25 does not say "preach to prisoners." It does not say "convert prisoners." It does not say "count crusade statistics." What it does say is *visit them.* Be a friend.

At times, prison ministry has been guilty of treating prisoners as objects of conversion. Conversion will come, God willing, if the prisoner sees something in you that he or she desires. But the way Jesus wants us to come to prisoners is through building a relationship; through seeing their needs and reaching out to help.

When you do share the truth with a prisoner, you are giving him or her an opportunity for change. Ultimately, however, the prisoner makes the choice. We are not any less successful if the prisoner rejects that opportunity. Once again, our role is faithfulness. After all, only one person knows the final number count of prison ministry, and that is God.

Prison ministry has often been compared to battle, and I think that comparison is fitting. Anyone who has really been on the frontlines knows that spiritual warfare is real. Ask Mother York, Bill Glass, Jack Murphy, or Chuck Colson. We need God's power. We need prayer support. Most of all we need the courage to be faithful, to take risks. Thomas Aquinas once observed that "if the primary aim of a captain were to preserve his ship, he'd keep it in the port forever."

The Message We Bring

All of us in jail and prison ministry know that because of overcrowding and violence and warehousing, jails and prisons don't change people for the better. We know that we are called to speak out against these dehumanizing conditions. But the single most powerful message we have to communicate is not about prison conditions.

On 9 May 1990, Pope John Paul II was touring part of Mexico City. Without even forewarning his security guard, he suddenly entered the closed prison yard of a maximum-security prison. It was a tough prison. Its inmates were mostly convicted murderers. And suddenly here was the Pope, surrounded by all these tough, hardened men. He said to them, "Don't lose hope. This is not the worst prison. *The worst prison is a closed heart.*"

That woman I heard crying in that church knew that only one thing could save her. The message of a risen Savior is what we bring to lost prisoners, whom we must see with God's eyes. We must see beyond a criminal offender's wretched state to his or her potential. It's a matter of perspective.

13

Building the Church
for Those in Prison

Charles W. Colson

It is fitting that the last chapter of this book be presented by a man whose name has become synonymous with prison ministry: Charles W. Colson. Mr. Colson, whose own life exemplifies dramatic conversion, is a powerfully gifted man who sees himself as a servant. He is clearly the leader of a great movement—not only in America, but internationally— to raise the social consciousness of both society and the church regarding ministry to prisoners.

Like the other speakers, Mr. Colson recognizes that the prison population and the problem of crime is growing out of control in our nation. He also makes an excellent case, quoting James Q. Wilson of the University of California, that crime is connected more to lack of spiritual values than it is to social conditions. And he uses examples of recent trips to the Soviet Union, Chino Prison in California, and Humaita Prison in Brazil to show how one-to-one contact with prisoners results in a life-changing difference.

For more than fifteen years, Charles Colson has led this great movement of prison ministry. He is uniquely qualified to exhort the church to be involved in prison ministry as a biblical mandate.

Five years ago I spoke at the closing session of the National Prison Ministry Conference about the importance of prison ministry. There were five hundred thousand people in our prison system then, and the United States was number three in the rate of incarceration per capita in the world, trailing only the Soviet Union and South Africa. Six years later, almost a million Americans are in prison. We are no longer number three. We no longer trail the Soviet Union or South Africa. Today we are number one in the world in the rate of incarceration.

Twenty-five percent of the black men in the inner cities are either in prison or on probation. Twenty-two thousand people will be murdered on the streets of American cities this year. During the one hundred hours of actual combat in the Persian Gulf War, more people were killed in American cities than in the Persian Gulf. A male between the ages of fourteen and twenty-one is more likely to be killed on inner-city streets today than if that same young man had been in the infantry in Vietnam.

Do we realize what is happening to us? The centers of our cities are falling right out from under us—and there is nothing the government can do about it. I don't care how many prisons they build. I don't care how many social programs they enact. There is nothing the government is going to do because the problem is like cancer in the heart of our cities. The only possible hope for doing anything in the city is the church. Are we going to turn our back on the problem and sit in our comfortable padded pews? Or are we going to go out and do what the church does best—share the love of Christ and bring men and women out of those environments to be transformed by Jesus Christ? Prison ministry is on the frontline of church service today, because prisons are the place where we are coming face-to-face with an evil that threatens to destroy us. And the church is the one power that can make a difference.

A Spiritual Problem—A Spiritual Solution

James Q. Wilson is a professor at University of California, formerly of Harvard. That name is familiar to all of you working in the prisons because he is probably the leading criminologist in America. A few years ago, James Q. Wilson was struck by an odd historical fact. He discovered that during the period of rapid industrialization in the middle of the nineteenth century, crime soared, but then it dropped about the time people were going into the mills—the very time you would think crime would be on the rise because of the urbanization of America. It started up again in the twenties, during a time of great prosperity, went down in the thirties, during the depression. And then in the sixties crime went soaring, and it's been soaring ever since.

Believing that poverty and social conditions were the cause of crime, Professor Wilson started to do a study to pinpoint exactly what was causing this up and down in crime. It wasn't poverty. During times of great poverty, crime actually dropped to its lowest levels, and it rose during periods of affluence.

Professor Wilson looked closer. He saw that during the second awakening in America, the Victorian era, when people were back in the churches, crime went down, despite the rapid urbanization of America. During the twenties, when the educated classes and the cultural elite began to believe Freud's teaching that all we had to do was tell people they were all right and we certainly wouldn't hold them accountable for their actions and their sins, crime started to rise. Then, despite the poverty in the thirties, crime started to go down again. In the sixties, and ever since, as America has rapidly become secularized, crime has increased. Professor Wilson concluded that there was a direct correlation between the level of spiritual activity and the level of crime. The more spiritual activity, the less crime; the less spiritual activity, the more crime.

What does that tell us about our society today? It tells us that if we live in a secular society, we can expect crime.

I was in the Soviet Union in the summer of 1990 as part of an official government delegation to visit prisons. The five of us went into four prisons no one in the West had ever visited before, including Perm Camp #45 in the Ural Mountains, where we also met with Vadim Petrovich Pocotny, the minister of internal affairs and the fourth-ranking official in the Soviet government at the time. He was a remarkably charismatic young leader.

We sat across the table as is customary in diplomatic sessions, with all the Americans on one side and all the Soviets on the other side. Mr. Pocotny welcomed us. He said there had been a 38 percent increase in crime in the Soviet Union last year, which he blamed on ethnic unrest, the economy, social factors, and political factors. Mike Quinlan, the leader of the delegation, responded to him, and the rest of the delegation responded in turn. We went down the line.

Finally, when my turn came, I said, "Mr. Minister, I appreciate your candor in talking about a 38 percent increase in crime. But if I may say so, respectfully, sir, I do not believe that the increase in crime is caused, as you believe, by social, ethnic, political, economic factors. That increase in crime was best diagnosed by your great novelist, Feodor Dostoyevsky, who wrote that classic of literature, *Brothers Karamatzov*. I went on to describe the scene where the unregenerate older brother is debating with the younger brother, a priest, over the sin of the middle brother. In the midst of one of the great debates over the source of evil and whether there could be a God in the world, the middle brother shouts out, "If there is no God, everything is permitted." Crime becomes inevitable.

I said, "Mr. Minister, the problem in the Soviet Union is not economic and social and political, it's the fact that you have had seventy years of atheism." I never thought I would see the day when I would be saying that to the fourth-ranking official of the Soviet government, sitting in the Kremlin.

He looked at me and he said, "Tell me about your ministry." I told him about Prison Fellowship and what we did in the prisons—taking the gospel of Jesus Christ to prisoners and seeing those men's lives changed. He looked at me and said, "Mr. Colson, that's exactly what we need here. Can you start Prison Fellowship in the Soviet Union?" And as we left, he said, with a twinkle in his eye, "God be with you."

Now don't get excited and say, "He was born again." He's still a hard-line communist who ran as one of the five candidates for president of Russia against Boris Yeltsin. But he's smart enough to realize something we are losing sight of in America—that you must have a strong religious base, or a society begins to collapse.

And that's the problem in America today—we're losing our religious base. That's why prison ministry is so important, because our job in prison ministry is to build the church.

A Vision for the Church

I had something of a vision. In the eighteen years since that fateful summer night when I gave my life to Christ in my friend's driveway, there have been four or five times that God has really shown me something in a powerful way. One of them was last fall. I was at the Chino Women's Prison, where twenty-five hundred inmates lived in a facility built for a thousand. I toured the prison before the rally at the end of a Prison Fellowship seminar. The gymnasium had been converted into a dormitory, a huge room with double-decker bunks right smack up against one another. Anybody who works in women's prisons (or men's prisons, for that matter) knows that homosexuality is a pervasive problem, but these bunks were right up against each other.

As we walked to the door, the women saw us, and they came from all corners and stood around us in a circle. One woman standing next to me had a can from the canteen that looked like soup with noodles, and she was eating from it. I asked, "Does that come from the mess hall?" She answered, "Oh, no, we can't eat the food in the mess hall. I saved up to have this. This is my treat. Once a week I buy a can from the canteen." She had eaten half of the soup, and she took a spoon out and held it up and said, "Would you like a taste of my food?" I thought about AIDS and all the things going on in the prison, but I realized what an offer of love that was, so of course I took it.

Later I toured death row. A woman named Maureen had been on death row for four months without a single visitor. I sat down on the floor in front of her cell and talked through the grate and told her about Jesus. Then I walked through the maximum-security section, where the guards all wear flak jackets because the women throw things out of their cells.

That afternoon we went out into the open compound to hold our final meeting. Jim Rowland, the former head of corrections for the state of California, and a great friend of Prison Fellowship, had said, "We are going to put up a big tent and have a tent rally in the middle of this prison." Sure enough, he had managed to erect a big yellow-and-white canvas tent. They announced the meeting over the loudspeakers, inviting people to come from the dormitories, and I saw the women begin pouring out of the buildings. There were four hundred chairs under this tent. The women filled the chairs almost immediately. Then they began to sit on the grass with some friends of Prison Fellowship who had come with us. I sat in the very back so I could watch what was happening during the preliminaries. Stormie Omartian, a wonderful gospel singer, was there sharing her testimony. From the back, I could see the women's heads nod as Stormy Omartian talked about having been abused by her father and left by her parents and locked in a closet and not given anything to eat for days at a time. These women were all nodding—they knew exactly what she was talking about.

Then I saw something I had never seen before. There was a center aisle in this tent, with chairs on both sides. And a woman inmate was walking up and down the center aisle with a roll of toilet paper. I've been in five hundred prisons, in forty countries, and I had seen just about everything, but I had never seen anyone carrying toilet paper up and down the aisle. I thought she might be reserving some seats—but no, all the seats were taken. Before long she went back to get another roll of toilet paper and kept on walking back and forth.

When it was my turn to speak to those inmates and I stood up before them, I saw what was going on. That woman was walking up and down that center aisle passing out toilet paper so those women could dry the tears of joy and repentance from their eyes. They were crying, and they didn't have any handkerchiefs.

There was a man with me, a businessman from Texas who had not been in a prison before. You know, there is one thing you never do in a prison: you never ask an inmate why he or she is in prison. But my friend sat right down next to one of the inmates and asked, "What are you here for?" She said, "Murder."

What do you say after that? "That's nice. Someone you knew? A friend?" "Murder" is a pretty good conversation stopper, but it didn't stop my friend. He asked how long her sentence was.

"Fifteen years to life," she said. "I cannot even be considered for parole for another eleven years."

She went on to say she was innocent, and from what my friend told me, she may well have been. My friend began to commiserate with the woman. "It must be tough."

"Oh, no!" she told him. "To live is Christ, to die is gain." And my friend said to me, all excited, "Isn't that beautiful: it's poetry." I replied, "It's not poetry. It was written by another prisoner in another prison cell two thousand years ago."

That day, as I stood on that platform, God gave me a vision for the church. I saw the church of Jesus Christ—people brought together, weeping, shedding tears of repentance and joy. And I had a vision for revival. But revival will only come to this land when our people are gathering at First Baptist or First Evangelical Free or St. Philip's or Second Presbyterian, or wherever it is and we're passing out toilet paper down the aisles of the church. It will only happen where people are testifying, "To live is Christ, to die is gain." Then there will be revival. And I saw it at Chino Women's Prison: I saw the church.

The Three Traps

The beauty of building the church inside these prisons is that in prison they don't fall for the three cultural traps into which I see the church falling today.

First, American Christians tend to look at the church as a building, a place—structure, bricks, mortar. But where in the New Testament is the church ever referred to as a building? At that incredible moment, the pivotal point of the drama of the New Testament, when Peter confesses his faith by saying to Jesus, "Thou art the Christ," what's the first thing Jesus does? He turns to Peter and says, "Peter, on this rock—your confession of faith— I will build my church" (Matt. 16:16–17, paraphrased). The word in Greek is *ekklesia,* that is, a gathering of people. Jesus wasn't talking about building a building; he was talking about building people. The church is the people of God. The greatest contribution Calvin made to the Reformation, in my opinion, was to reestablish the notion that the church is not an institution; the church is the *people.* It is interesting that there aren't any church buildings in prisons. They don't get hung up on that. They know what the church is. The church is their brothers and sisters. The community of saints, as it was called in the first century. The people of God.

Second, men and women in prison don't get hung up on the church as a place for therapy, a place to be made to feel good. A church in Indianapolis has a great big sign out front that says, "Come worship with us; we'll make you feel better." When did Jesus tell people church would make them feel better? A church in Denver, Colorado, just changed its name; it calls itself the "Happy Church." But the job of the church is not to make people happy; it's to make people holy. We run marketing surveys to find out what will bring people into church, and so we give it to them: something that will get them through the week, something that will make them feel good.

A *USA Today* poll last year asked people why they go to church. Forty-five percent of the respondents said, "Because it's good for you." Twenty-six percent said, "For pleasure." Twenty-one percent said, "For peace of mind." No wonder the New Age is the fastest growing religion in America. If the purpose of the church is just to make you feel good, if all we as Christians have to offer people is a place where they can come and worship some unknown God, then the New Age will always beat us. After all, the New Age tells people they can be God—and what would feel better than that? Why worship God when you can *be* God?

The tragedy is that even Christians are lining the pews of our churches with people who are there because they want to be made to feel good, to get through the rest of the week. We should be ashamed. We do not worship God because it feels good. We worship God, in the words of the Hartford Declaration of 1975, because God is to be worshiped. In prison we find that sense of worship.

Worshiping with the women at Chino Women's Prison was one of the richest experiences I have ever had. Those believers were worshipful. They were serious. They were loving God. They weren't there to be told that they could feel good. How do you feel good when you are facing eleven more years before you can even be considered for parole? No, in prison you face the reality of your own sin. You repent, and you feel the incomparable joy of knowing that your sins have been forgiven—that you can live for Christ or die for gain. There is no therapy gospel in the prisons.

The third mistake I think the church makes is to acquaint success with bigness and growth. As if buses and budgets and baptisms and buildings and bigness mattered. Nowhere in the Scripture is size shown to be a measure of the church's success.

Certainly, when Pentecost came and the first Christians preached with power, God added thousands to his church. When God creates growth, that's wonderful. The tragedy comes when we look at the church and assume we are not doing the job right unless we are growing. Pastors are under tremendous pressure to grow at all costs. And that means they had better preach a popular message because their object is recruitment, not repentance. No wonder we have "Happy Churches." What an abomination!

John Wesley said he could shake the foundations of hell and change England if he had a hundred people who loved God and hated sin. I'd rather have a hundred people who love God and hate sin than ten thousand sitting in the pews waiting for their ears to be tickled.

But there is no room in the prisons to worry about growth. They are worried about simply hanging on. They are fighting the sin and evil and depravity all around them. They are not worried about getting bigger sanctuaries. They are worried about surviving with each other. And that's why prison churches are so exciting.

People ask me, "Where do you like most to preach?" I've spoken twice in the House of Commons and the Parliament in England. I've spoken at the luncheon that follows the National Prayer Breakfast in our own country. I've spoken three or four times in the Congress to different groups at their prayer breakfast meeting. I've been to all the Governors' Prayer Breakfasts. But let me into those prisons any day to preach. That's where people have lost it all and can say, as Solzhenitsyn said, "I never was free in my life until I lost everything. Now I've discovered the one thing that mattered." That's a church where I want to preach.

To Build the Church

So what is our task? Those of us who are called by God to bring the gospel into prison are called to help build the church. We have nothing else to offer but to hold our hands out and say, "Let us help you build the church here. And as you get out of prison, let us help you into the church."

I think we evangelicals—particularly those of us in the parachurch movement—make a mistake when we put evangelism as the first call of the church. Every conference, every book, every speaker seems to agree that evangelism is the first call of the church. But we equate evangelism with presenting people with the gospel and then asking them to accept it. And if they make that decision, we act as if that's all we care about, as if our job were done.

But our calling goes beyond that. Scripture tells us to "Go therefore and make disciples of all the nations, baptizing them in the name of the Father and the Son and the Holy Spirit, teaching them to observe all that I commanded you" (Matt. 28:19–20 NASB). That is more than just proclaiming the gospel. The idea that we can lead people to make decisions for Christ and then leave them alone with their new faith is wrong. You cannot evangelize outside of the church, because you can't fulfill the Great Commission apart from the church.

When Peter made his confession of faith, saying, "Thou art the Christ," Jesus did not say, "That's wonderful Peter; you are now saved." He said, "On that confession, on that rock, I will build my church."

The response to a confession of faith is to "build the church." God has made you a member based on your confession of faith. You are automatically in. And anyone who has made the same confession is in with you. Your job then is to begin discipling, to bring people to baptism, to help others grow in Christ, to teach them all that Jesus taught his apostles.

Look what happened after Pentecost. Peter had preached with such power that people came up to him and asked, "What must we do?" Peter said, "Repent, and let each of you be baptized in the name of Jesus Christ for the forgiveness of your sins; and you shall receive the gift of the Holy Spirit" (Acts 2:37–38 NASB). And that's what they did. They gathered together, "continually devoting themselves to the apostles' teaching and to fellowship, to the breaking of bread and to prayer (v. 42 NASB).

When people make a confession of faith, they become part of the body of Christ. The Presbyterian Church in western North Carolina has agreed to offer associate church membership to inmates. And an inmate who becomes an associate member of the church inside the prison is given full membership when he or she comes back into the community. These Presbyterians are discipling inmates in the church. They are building the church. And that's the only way we can possibly manage as prison ministers. Our job is to bring those men and women in that prison into discipleship and fellowship in the body of Christ.

"I Will Build *My* Church"

We have the sin of presumption in the American church. We give people our simple little formulas and figure we have done our job as Christians. But remember whose church it is. It is not our church or my church or your church or Chuck Swindoll's church or Bill Hybel's church. Jesus said "I will build *my* church." He calls people from every background, every confession, every color, and every race, and he calls them to himself as his body.

I love the story Irina Roskoskay tells. Irina Roskoskay is a marvelous Russian poet who was imprisoned for four years in the Soviet Union because her poetry talked about God and human dignity. She was released the night before Reagan and Gorbachev met in Iceland because there had been so much pressure built up around the world. I've gotten to know Irina very well over these last years. Do you know how she became a Christian? She became a Christian because as a child in school she had to go to indoctrination classes where week after week she was taught that there is no God. And she thought to herself, "If they are working so hard to teach me that there isn't a God, there must be a God." She began to pray. And she began to understand that God loved her so much that he would die for her.

Then Irina began to read Russian literature—Dostoyevsky and Pushkin and Tolstoy. And in her reading she slowly saw an outline of Christ and she became a Christian. She never had a Bible in her hand. Nobody ever witnessed to her. But she came to love Jesus. When she was twenty-one years old, a Jew came up to her and said, "I'd like to give you a Bible." She read the New Testament and said, "Wow, that's him! That's the one I've been worshiping."

Christ says, "*I* will build my church." We don't have to worry about that. "I, Jesus, will build my people on their confession of faith." Our job is to build the body so that people can come—even out of prison—and be part of that body and be loved by that body and be discipled and taught all that Jesus commanded us to teach them. That is what it means to fulfill the Great Commission.

The Secret of Humaita

Humaita Prison in Brazil is a remarkable place. Almost twenty years ago, it was a rotting building where prisoners were tortured. Then three Christian men went to the government and asked permission to take over the prison. They got permission. And they started to run Humaita as a Christian prison. They did not restrict it to Christian inmates, but you couldn't stay there very long without coming to know Christ.

When an inmate arrives with handcuffs on, they take off the handcuffs and say, "In this prison you will no longer be chained by steel; you will be chained by the love of Christ."

They assign people to a buddy system. Each new inmate is assigned to an elder who loves the Lord.

And at every single meal, they stand before the meal and recite The Lord's Prayer in Portuguese.

If anyone ever asks whether Christ makes a difference, send them down to San Jose des Campos in Brazil to the Humaita Prison. For all those years, while the government of Brazil has had a 74 percent recidivism rate, Humaita has released more than three hundred inmates, and they have had only twelve come back. That's 4 percent recidivism.

One inmate showed me Humaita's secret. This inmate was convicted for murder, but he was my guide through the prison, walking around with all the prison keys hanging from his belt. He asked whether I'd like to see the maximum security cell. So we walked down a long hall of steel doors toward the cell in question. He said it used to be the punishment cell where they tortured people. "We still use it for punishment," he said. "We have one inmate in there."

He took me to the door and looked through the little peek hole. "Are you sure you want to go in there?" he asked. "I have been in maximum security holes all over the world," I told him. I wanted to see. He said, "Okay," and then unlocked the door. As he swung the door open, I looked in and saw a couple of chairs and a dim light and flowers on the table. I walked through the door. To the right I saw a crucifix—Christ hanging on the cross.

My guide pointed to the image of Christ and said, "This is the prisoner who is taking the punishment for us." A sign on the wall above the crucifix said, "We are together" in Portuguese. They understand that they are joined with Christ, who suffered.

We have to remember what our call is as ministers. When we go into those prisons, we have to remember that we go for one reason—as servants of Christ. It's all any of us have any claim to be. We don't go in arrogant and haughty, as if we have all the answers. We go in to serve suffering people, as Jesus served us.

I love the words that Paul wrote from his prison cell:

> Have this attitude in yourselves which was also in Christ Jesus, who, although He existed in the form of God, did not regard equality with God a thing to be grasped, but emptied Himself, taking the form of a bond-servant, and being made in the likeness of men. And being found in appearance as a man, He humbled Himself by becoming obedient to the point of death, even death on the cross. (Phil. 2:5–8 NASB)

If you dare say that you are a minister of the gospel, you must have in you this mind which was in Christ Jesus. Though he could have grasped equality with God, he did not, but emptied himself out as a love offering for the world. That's the kind of people we have to be.

People who are proud and self-assured, confident and cocky, and maybe a little haughty are usually far away from God. When you come into the presence of God, as the reformer said, you come into the presence of the holy, majestic, almighty, all-powerful Creator, who gives you every breath to breathe. That should drive you to your knees and make you humble! When I watch people who exude humility, I know they've got to be on their knees every morning close to God. That's the kind of people we need to be.

God, give us the will to build a church, to know that it is not ours but belongs to Jesus. We are but living stones, a foundation of people. Give us the courage to stand for truth, to be able to speak truth in love. And then give us humility to serve the one who suffered for us and by whose grace we can know life everlasting. Amen.

Epilogue

On 22 June 1980, Alvin Lee King, a forty-five-year-old math teacher, entered the First Baptist Church in Daingerfield, Texas. "This is war!" he cried out, then he shot sixteen people.

The tragedy was real, but King's exclamation was also symbolic. For we are truly in the midst of a war—a spiritual war in which the enemy seeks to keep offenders in the clutches of sin, and a war of crime that is raging in our cities.

The good news is, of course, that we're on the winning side. As the church of Jesus Christ, we have the responsibility to show compassion for prisoners and to bring them the message that, in Christ, their lives really can change.

Prison ministry is the great and only hope of transforming the hearts of offenders. Without a change of heart, the recidivism rate will continue to soar in America. The great majority of those released from prison will return to crime. The failure rate among juvenile offenders is over 85 percent. The failure rate among adult offenders is over 75 percent.

But when prisoners are offered the good news of Jesus Christ, when volunteers visit, nurture, and disciple prisoners, when someone offers them a viable support system upon their release, and when the church welcomes them, the success rate is often 60 to 80 percent. This is the reverse of what government can do.

Government is not equipped to transform offenders from the inside out. All our social scientists and psychologists can testify that no extraordinary measures or controls from the outside can change an offender's behavior in a lasting way. But God can.

That, of course, is the message of this book. All of its authors have stated clearly that God alone is the source of true justice, the impetus of all good change. They have also articulated that compassion for both offenders and victims is a biblical mandate.

Many of these authors have spoken prophetically. All have spoken from years of experience and hearts of compassion. And every author has challenged the reader, using the authority of the Bible as the basis for a call to increase voluntarism in prison ministry.

Our public school system spends $4,713 per pupil per year, and the average starting salary for a teacher is $19,000. Yet our government spends an average of $20,000 per prisoner per year, and the cost of keeping an inmate in prison is more than the tuition of the finest schools in America, including Harvard, Yale, and MIT. From an economic standpoint alone, the church must help turn this terrible tide of crime that is ravaging our cities and communities.

But of course our motivation is much deeper than economic. As forgiven sinners ourselves, and as Christ's followers, we are called to be bearers of the light, even to the darkest places, even to the prisons. Each church and each Christian in his or her own way should seek to help support jail and prison ministry.